Oxford Primary Illustrated Maths Dictionary

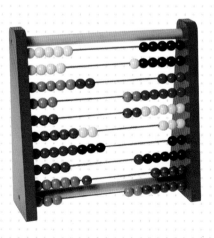

Compiled by
Peter Patill

D1611102

OXFORD
UNIVERSITY PRESS

OXFORD
UNIVERSITY PRESS

Great Clarendon Street, Oxford, OX2 6DP, United Kingdom

Oxford University Press is a department of the University of Oxford.
It furthers the University's objective of excellence in research,
scholarship, and education by publishing worldwide. Oxford is a
registered trade mark of Oxford University Press in the UK and in
certain other countries

British Library Cataloguing in Publication Data

Data available

ISBN: 978 0 19 277247 3
10 9 8 7 6 5 4 3 2 1

Printed in China

Paper used in the production of this book is a natural,
recyclable product made from wood grown in sustainable forests.
The manufacturing process conforms to the environmental
regulations of the country of origin.

The publishers would like to thank Paul Broadbent and
Andrew Delahunty for their contributions to this edition.

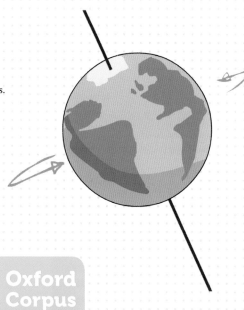

Oxford OWL

For school
Discover eBooks, inspirational
resources, advice and support

For home
Helping your child's learning
with free eBooks, essential
tips and fun activities

www.oxfordowl.co.uk

Oxford Corpus

You can trust this dictionary
to be up to date, relevant
and engaging because
it is powered by the
Oxford Corpus, a unique
living database of children's
and adults' language.

Contents

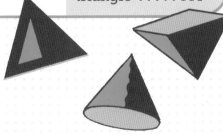

⚙ Introduction 4

⚙ Symbols and short forms 6

⚙ A-Z 7-117

⚙ Shapes 118

⚙ Useful mathematical tables 119

⚙ Useful mathematical formulae 119

⚙ Time 120

⚙ Instruction words and phrases 122

⚙ Chance words 123

⚙ Money words 123

⚙ Position and direction words 124

⚙ Apparatus 126

Panels

angle 9

average 12

axis 12

chart 19

circle 20

data 29

diagram 34

fraction 45

graph 48

number 74

polygon 85

polyhedron . . . 86

prism 87

pyramid 89

set 97

symmetry . . . 105

triangle 111

Introduction

The *Oxford Primary Illustrated Maths Dictionary* contains over 1,000 words and phrases. A wide range of mathematical terms are presented in alphabetical order with clear definitions and related words which help to build subject vocabulary in young learners.

With words from the curriculum and detailed vocabulary associated with graphs, fractions, shapes and measures, this book is designed to be a comprehensive quick reference guide for both the classroom and the home.

catch words

show the first and last word on the page and guide you to the correct place to find the word you need

headword

is in alphabetical order, in blue

other forms

show you how to spell different forms of the word, such as plurals or past forms

Word Build panel

shows other words which work together with the headword in the same topic area

illustration

helps to show the meaning of the word

cross-reference

points you to the main entry which gives you the definition of the word

---

average to axis

average

The average is a number that best represents a set of numbers. There are different ways of determining a representative number: mean, median and mode.

WORD BUILD

➤ **mean**

Mean is a kind of average. To find the mean, total the quantities then divide by the number of quantities.

see also range

➤ **median**

Median is a kind of average. To find the median, write out the quantities in order. The median is the quantity that has the middle value.

see also range

➤ **mode**

Mode is a kind of average. The mode is the quantity or number that occurs most often.

EXAMPLE

Here are five numbers ranging from 3 to 9

3   3   4   6   9

The **mean** is 5 because (3 + 3 + 4 + 6 + 9) ÷ 5 equals 5.

The **median** is 4 because it is the middle value.

The **mode** is 3 because it occurs most often.

average speed *see* speed

axis (*plural* axes)

❶ Many graphs have two axes: a horizontal axis and a vertical axis.

vertical axis

origin

horizontal axis

see also graph, origin

○ **x-axis**

The horizontal axis of a graph is called the x-axis.

○ **y-axis**

The vertical axis of a graph is called the y-axis.

❷ An axis is a straight line through the middle of a 3D shape. The Earth turns on its axis.

axis

see also axis of rotation, symmetry

12

Where a word has several meanings, different meanings are numbered and often other related words are listed. This is a great way to build and extend vocabulary. Green and yellow panels bring together in one place words that are related to the headword or can be used together with it to talk or write about a topic. Illustrations also help to explain the meaning.

The thematic supplement explores in more detail some of the key mathematical terms and concepts in focus areas, as well as the instructional words and phrases that children are likely to find in their maths textbooks, worksheets and tests.

Rr

radius *see* circle

random
Random means purely by chance. If you choose a number at random you pick any number that you wish. Random numbers do not have an order.
➤ **randomly**
Randomly means at random or purely by chance.

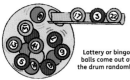
Lottery or bingo balls come out of the drum randomly.

range
The range is the difference between the smallest value and the largest value. You often need to know the range when you are finding averages.

▶ EXAMPLE

3   3   4   6   9

Here are five numbers from 3 to 9.

The smallest number is 3, the largest is 9.

The **range** is from 3 to 9 which equals 6.

see also average

rate
Rate is a measure of how quickly an amount changes compared to another. It is also a measure of how quickly an event happens.

▶ EXAMPLE

Water flows from a hose at a faster **rate** than from a tap.

If it takes 1 hour to drive 60 km, the **rate** at which the journey was completed is 60 km/h (60 kilometres per hour).

ratio
A ratio is a way of comparing one quantity to another. The sign for ratio is **:** .

The ratio of cars to motorbikes is 3:2 or $\frac{3}{2}$.

◯ **equivalent ratio**
Equivalent ratios give the same value for each ratio when one part is compared to the other.

White and blue paint that is mixed in the ratios of 2:3 and 4:6 are **equivalent ratios** so would give the same colour mix.

see also proportion

a b c d e f g h i j k l m n o p q r s t u v w x y z

91

definition
shows what the word means and if a word has more than one meaning, then each meaning is numbered

derivative
shows you an additional word from the same family as the headword

example
shows how you might use a word and helps you understand the meaning

alphabet
the alphabet is given on every page with the letter you are in highlighted so you can find your way around the dictionary easily

related words panel
points you to other words that help to explain this word or build more knowledge in this topic area

other related words
point you to other words that help to explain this word or build more knowledge in this topic area

Symbols and short forms

+	plus, add, positive		2D	two-dimensional
−	minus, subtract, negative		3D	three-dimensional
×	multiplied by		g	gram
÷	divided by		kg	kilogram
$\sqrt{}$	square root		mm	millimetre
$\sqrt[3]{}$	cube root		cm	centimetre
°	degree		m	metre
=	equals		dm	decimetre
≠	is not equal to		km	kilometre
≈	is approximately equal to		ml	millilitre
<	is less than		cl	centilitre
>	is greater than		l	litre
≤	is less than or equal to		dl	decilitre
≥	is greater than or equal to		r	remainder, radius
%	percentage		°C	degrees Celsius
∞	infinity		°F	degrees Fahrenheit
⇉	parallel		mm^2	square millimetres
⊥	perpendicular		cm^2	square centimetres
π	pi, 3.142, $\frac{22}{7}$		m^2	square metres
			km^2	square kilometres

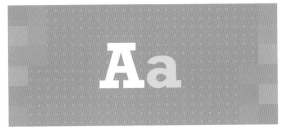

Aa

abacus (*plural* abacuses, abaci)

An abacus is a counting frame with beads or rings used to help count, calculate and read the value of numbers.

accurate

When you are accurate you are exactly right without any mistakes or errors.

2 cm

This measurement is accurate to the nearest cm.

➤ **accuracy**

The accuracy of something is how exactly right it is. When you use measuring instruments you measure to a certain accuracy. For example, you might measure to the nearest millimetre, gram or millilitre.

acute angle *see* angle

acute-angled triangle *see* triangle

addend

Addends are any numbers that are added together to make a total.

▮▮▶	EXAMPLE
$8 + 6 = 14$	
8 and 6 are **addends**.	

addition

Addition is combining two or more numbers together to make a new number called the sum. The symbol for addition is **+**. This is called the plus sign.

➤ **add**

To add numbers together is to combine them to make a new number called a sum.

▮▮▶	EXAMPLE
These are all the same **addition**.	
$4 + 7 = 11$	
The sum of 4 and 7 is 11.	
Four plus seven equals eleven.	
Four add seven equals eleven.	
The total of 4 and 7 is 11.	
7 added to 4 makes 11.	
Adding 7 to 4 totals 11.	

see also operation, plus, sum, total

adjacent

Adjacent means lying next to, or side by side.

These two angles are adjacent to each other.

see also parallel

afternoon

The time between noon and evening is called the afternoon.

3:00 p.m.

three o'clock in the afternoon

see also evening, morning, p.m.

algebra

Algebra is the branch of mathematics that uses symbols or letters to represent numbers.

➤ **algebraic**

An algebraic equation or formula is one that uses algebra.

EXAMPLE
We can use **algebra** to work out the area of different sized rectangles.
The area (a) of rectangles is length (l) multiplied by width (w).
The formula for the area of rectangles is $a = l \times w$.

see also equation, formula

algorithm

An algorithm is the method you use to work out the answer to a calculation.

EXAMPLE
53×5

- Multiply the tens first: $50 \times 5 = 250$
- Then multiply the ones: $3 \times 5 = 15$
- Then total the two parts: $250 + 15 = 265$

see also calculation

a.m.

The letters a.m. stand for *ante meridiem*, which is Latin for 'before noon'. The letters are used to show times after 12 midnight but before 12 noon.

3:00 a.m.

three o'clock in the morning

see also morning, night, p.m.

amount

An amount is the total quantity of a set of items.

EXAMPLE
The total **amount** of money in my purse is £5.20.

see also total

analogue

Analogue clocks and watches have hands that tell the time.

Analogue watches have hands.

Digital watches only have numbers.

see also digital clock

angle

angle

An angle is an amount of turn. Angles can be measured in degrees.

acute angle

see also degree, vertex

⚙ acute angle

An acute angle is an angle that is less than a right angle. It is any angle between 0° and 90°.

⚙ exterior angle

An exterior angle at any vertex is 180° minus the interior angle.

see also polygon, vertex

⚙ flat angle

A flat angle is two right angles together. It is an angle of 180°.

⚙ interior angle

An interior angle is the angle formed inside a polygon between two adjacent edges.

see also polygon

⚙ obtuse angle

An obtuse angle measures between 90° and 180°.

⚙ reflex angle

A reflex angle is an angle that is between 180° and 360°.

⚙ right angle

A right angle is a quarter of a complete turn. It measures 90°.

⚙ straight angle

A straight angle is half a turn. It is two right angles and looks like a straight line.

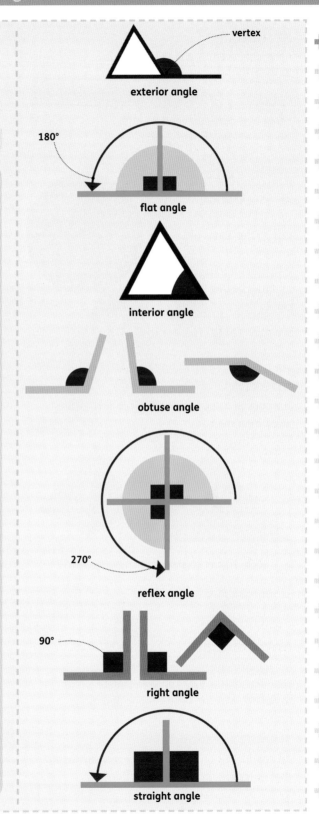

vertex

exterior angle

180°

flat angle

interior angle

obtuse angle

270°

reflex angle

90°

right angle

straight angle

a b c d e f g h i j k l m n o p q r s t u v w x y z

A B C D E F G H I J K L M N O P Q R S T U V W X Y Z

annual

An annual event is one that takes place every year.

EXAMPLE

Your birthday is an **annual** event.

anticlockwise

Anticlockwise means turning the opposite way to the hands of a clock.

OPPOSITE The opposite of anticlockwise is clockwise.

see also **clockwise, rotate**

apex (*plural* apexes, apices)

The apex of a shape is the point that is furthest away from the base.

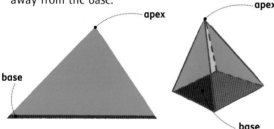

apex

apex

base

base

Both 2D and 3D shapes can have apexes.

see also **base, vertex**

approximate

An approximate number or measurement is near enough the exact answer. Similar words to approximate are nearly, round about and near enough.

➤ approximation

An approximation is a number or measurement that is nearly right but not exact.

➤ approximately

Approximately means roughly but not exactly. The symbol for approximately equal to is ≈.

EXAMPLE

3.99m ≈ 4.00m
3.99 metres is **approximately** 4 metres.

$200.01 ≈ $200
$200.01 is **approximately** $200.

£0.99 ≈ £1·00
£0.99 is **approximately** £1.00.

see also **estimate, round**

arc see circle

area

The area of a shape is how much surface it has. Area is measured in square units such as square centimetres (cm²), square metres (m²) and square kilometres (km²).

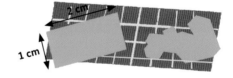

2 cm

1 cm

Both shapes have an area of 2 cm2 .

see also **perimeter, volume**

arithmetic

Arithmetic is working with numbers. It includes adding, subtracting, multiplying and dividing with whole numbers, fractions and decimals. »

If you are good at **arithmetic** you will be able to work out the answers to these calculations in your head.

| 34 + 67 | 24 × 5 |
| 72 – 39 | 120 ÷ 4 |

Answers: 34 + 67 = 101   4 × 5 = 120
72 – 39 = 33   120 ÷ 4 = 30

see also calculation, operation

array

An array is an arrangement of numbers or objects into a rectangle. The rows and columns of an array are used to help work out totals in multiplication problems.

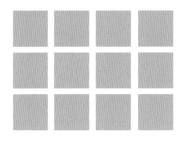

This array shows that 4 × 3 and 3 × 4 both equal 12.

see also multiply, multiplication

ascending

Ascending means going up or increasing in size.

 OPPOSITE The opposite of ascending is descending.

EXAMPLE

2   6   16   29   45

These numbers are in **ascending** order.

see also descending

associative law

The associative law states that when you add or multiply any three or more numbers, the answer does not depend on how the pairs are grouped.

EXAMPLE

Addition:
(a + b) + c = a + (b + c)
(4 + 5) + 6 = 4 + (5 + 6)

Multiplication:
(a × b) × c = a × (b × c)
(5 × 3) × 2 = 5 × (3 × 2)

Subtraction and division are not **associative**.

see also commutative law, distributive law

asymmetrical

A shape is asymmetrical if it has no lines of symmetry.

This shape has no lines of symmetry so it is asymmetrical.

see also symmetry

attribute

An attribute is a property such as colour, shape, size, number of sides or type of angle.

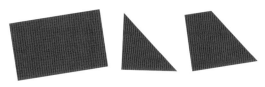

The attributes these shapes have in common include: colour, right-angled, straight-sided.

The attributes they do not have in common include: number of sides, area, symmetry.

see also property

average

The average is a number that best represents a set of numbers. There are different ways of determining a representative number: mean, median and mode.

WORD BUILD

➤ mean

Mean is a kind of average. To find the mean, total the quantities then divide by the number of quantities.

see also range

➤ median

Median is a kind of average. To find the median, write out the quantities in order. The median is the quantity that has the middle value.

see also range

➤ mode

Mode is a kind of average. The mode is the quantity or number that occurs most often.

EXAMPLE

Here are five numbers ranging from 3 to 9

$$3 \quad 3 \quad 4 \quad 6 \quad 9$$

The **mean** is 5 because $(3 + 3 + 4 + 6 + 9) \div 5$ equals 5.

The **median** is 4 because it is the middle value.

The **mode** is 3 because it occurs most often.

average speed *see* speed

axis (*plural* axes)

❶ Many graphs have two axes: a horizontal axis and a vertical axis.

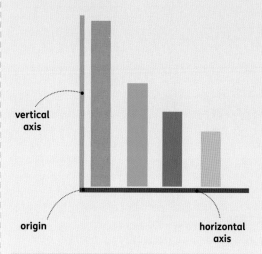

vertical axis

origin

horizontal axis

see also graph, origin

⚙ x-axis

The horizontal axis of a graph is called the x-axis.

⚙ y-axis

The vertical axis of a graph is called the y-axis.

❷ An axis is a straight line through the middle of a 3D shape. The Earth turns on its axis.

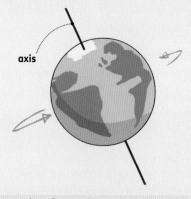

axis

see also axis of rotation, symmetry

axis of rotation

An axis of rotation is a straight line through the middle of a 3D shape around which the shape turns.

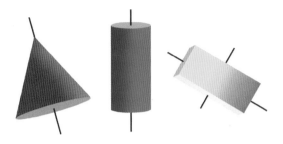

some axes of rotation on 3D shapes

see also rotate, symmetry, three-dimensional shape

Bb

balance

❶ A balance is an instrument for weighing or comparing masses or weights.

a balance

see also scale

❷ A balance is the amount of money that is still owing or how much remains.

 EXAMPLE

If you have $100 in the bank and withdraw $20 the **balance** is $80.

see also interest

❸ An equation balances when one side equals the other.

 EXAMPLE

$3 + b = 12$
For this equation to **balance**, b must equal 9.

see also equation

bar chart (also bar graph) see chart

bar-line graph see graph

bar model

A bar model is a representation of a problem using rectangle bars or boxes to help make sense of the problem.

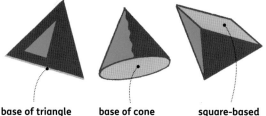

| Emma | 14 |
| James | 9 | ? |

James has 9 stickers and his sister Emma has 14 stickers. How many more stickers does Emma have than James?

base

❶ The base of a shape is the part on which it stands. It is usually the horizontal part but not always.

base of triangle   base of cone   square-based pyramid

see also pyramid

❷ Our number system is called base 10 because we use 10 digits to record all numbers. Base 10 numbers are grouped by ones, tens, hundreds and so on. Other number systems use a different base. For example, base 2 numbers would only use the digits 0 and 1.

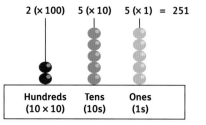

2 ($\times$ 100)   5 ($\times$ 10)   5 ($\times$ 1) = 251

| Hundreds (10 × 10) | Tens (10s) | Ones (1s) |

base ten

see also place value, binary

bearing

A bearing is an amount of turn measured from North in a clockwise direction. Bearings are used with maps to work out travelling directions.

North

bearing 045°

North

bearing 135°

North

bearing 315°

see also compass

billion

A billion is a thousand million. A billion used to mean a million million (1,000,000,000,000) but this is not used in maths anymore.

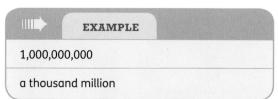

| ▐▐▐▶ | EXAMPLE |

1,000,000,000

a thousand million

see also million

binary

Binary means made of two different things.
Binary numbers are made of 1s and 0s.
Binary numbers are in base 2.

> **EXAMPLE**
>
> The **binary** numbers equivalent to the first 8 decimal numbers are:
>
> | 1 | 2 | 3 | 4 | 5 | 6 | 7 | 8 |
> |---|---|---|-----|-----|-----|-----|------|
> | 1 | 10 | 11 | 100 | 101 | 110 | 111 | 1000 |

see also base

bisect

When you bisect something, you cut it in half.

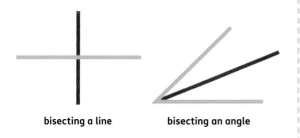

bisecting a line   bisecting an angle

block graph *see* graph

brackets

Brackets tell you which part of a calculation to work out first. They look like this: **( )**.

> **EXAMPLE**
>
> 12 – **(7 – 3)**
> 12 – 4 = 8
>
> **(2 × 3)** + 4
> 6 + 4 = 10

see also calculation, order of operations

breadth

The breadth is the distance from one side to the other. It is sometimes called the width. When measuring length and breadth, the breadth is usually the shorter length.

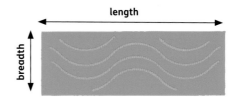

see also length, width

British Summer Time (*also* BST)

British Summer Time (BST) is the period of time between March and October when clocks are put forward by 1 hour in the UK.

> **EXAMPLE**
>
> In the UK, what is 4 p.m. in October becomes 3 p.m. in November when the clocks are put back by 1 hour, from **British Summer Time** to Greenwich Mean Time.

see also Greenwich Mean Time

C

The Romans used the letter C to stand for the number 100.

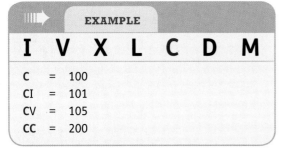

EXAMPLE

I	V	X	L	C	D	M

C	=	100
CI	=	101
CV	=	105
CC	=	200

see also Roman numerals

calculation

A calculation is when you have to work out the answer to a number problem.

➤ **calculate**

To calculate something is to work out the answer to a number problem.

EXAMPLE

Calculate the answer to: $\frac{3}{4}$ of 160.

Answer: 120

see also arithmetic, operation

calculator

A calculator is a machine that works out calculations very rapidly and accurately.

display
memory key
operation key
number key

see also operation

calendar

A calendar shows time divided into years, months, weeks and days.

see also leap year, day, week, month, year

cancel

To cancel a fraction you divide the numerator and denominator by the same number. Cancelling lets you simplify a fraction into smaller numbers that are easier to work with.

EXAMPLE

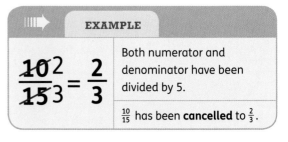

$$\frac{\cancel{10}^2}{\cancel{15}_3} = \frac{2}{3}$$

Both numerator and denominator have been divided by 5.

$\frac{10}{15}$ has been **cancelled** to $\frac{2}{3}$.

see also fraction, denominator, numerator, reduce, simplify

capacity

Capacity is how much something holds. It is usually measured in litres and millilitres.

The capacity of the carton is 2 litres.

see also litre, millilitre, volume

cardinal number *see* number

Carroll diagram *see* diagram

Celsius

Celsius is a scale used to measure temperature. It is written as degrees Celsius (°C). It is named after the Swedish scientist Anton Celsius. It has replaced the Centigrade scale.

 EXAMPLE

Water freezes at 0°**C** and boils at 100°**C** on the **Celsius** scale.

see also centigrade, Fahrenheit

cent

A cent is a unit of money used in some countries. It is $\frac{1}{100}$ of the value of the main unit of currency.

 EXAMPLE

There are 100 **cents** in a US dollar.

centi-

Centi- is used as a prefix to show the number $\frac{1}{100}$.

 EXAMPLE

A centimetre is $\frac{1}{100}$ of a metre.

see also milli-

centigrade

Centigrade is a scale used to measure temperature. It is the same scale as Celsius (°C) which is now used instead of centigrade.

 EXAMPLE

Water freezes at 0°C and boils at 100°C on the **centigrade** and Celsius scale.

see also Celsius, Fahrenheit

centilitre (*also* cl)

A centilitre is one hundredth of a litre. There are 10 millilitres in 1 centilitre. Centi- at the start of a word usually means 'one hundredth'. The short way of writing centilitre is cl.

EXAMPLE

100 **centilitres** = 1 litre

100 **cl** = 1 l

1 **centilitre** = 10 millilitres

1 **cl** = 10 ml

1 **centilitre** = $\frac{1}{100}$ litre = 10 millilitres

see also centi-, decilitre, litre, millilitre

a
b
c
d
e
f
g
h
i
j
k
l
m
n
o
p
q
r
s
t
u
v
w
x
y
z

centimetre (*also* cm)

A centimetre is one hundredth of a metre. There are 10 millimetres in 1 centimetre. Centi- at the start of a word usually means 'one hundredth'.

⏩	**EXAMPLE**
100 **centimetres** = 1 metre
100 **cm** = 1 m
1 **centimetre** = 10 millimetres
1 **cm** = 10 mm
1 **centimetre** = $\frac{1}{100}$ metre = 10 millimetres

see also centi-, metre, millimetre

centre

The centre of a shape is exactly in its middle.

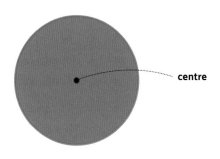

centre

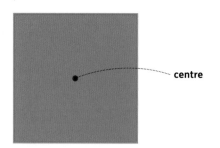

centre

see also circle

centre of rotation

Shapes can be rotated clockwise or anticlockwise about a point. The point can be inside the shape or outside the shape. This point is called the centre of rotation.

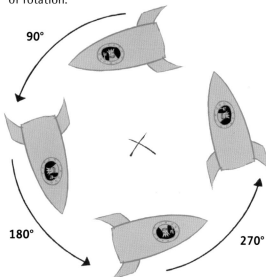

90°
180°
270°

X is the centre of rotation of the rocket.

see also symmetry

century

A century is a set of one hundred. A century is 100 years.

Roman soldiers were organized into hundreds. They were called centurions.

see also millennium year

chart

A chart shows information in an orderly way.

see also graph, tally

⚙ bar chart (*also* bar graph)

A bar chart (or bar graph) is a graph that uses bars to show information. The bars are all the same thickness and can be horizontal or vertical. The bars usually show two different types of information. For example, to show how many animals there are, the bars can have names listed on the x-axis and numbers on the y-axis. Vertical bar charts or bar graphs are also called column graphs.

see also axis, graph, histogram

⚙ pie chart

In a pie chart information is shown as a circle. The different-sized sectors or slices of the pie chart stand for the different quantities they represent. For example, the slices of a pie chart can represent the percentage of people ordering different types of dessert in a restaurant.

see also circle

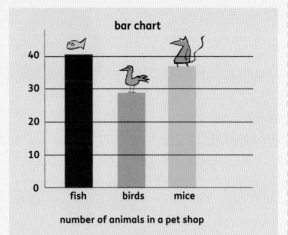

bar chart

number of animals in a pet shop

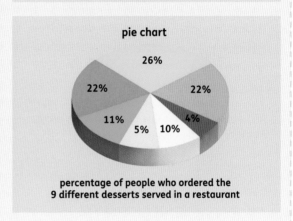

pie chart

percentage of people who ordered the 9 different desserts served in a restaurant

---

chord *see* circle

chronological

Items or events in chronological order are put in order of time, starting with the earliest.

> **EXAMPLE**

These Summer Olympic years are in **chronological** order:

- Beijing 2008

- London 2012

- Rio 2016

- Tokyo 2020

➤ chronology

Chronology is the order of time in which events happen, starting with the earliest time.

> **EXAMPLE**

Can you list these months in the correct **chronology**?

- April

- February

- November

- June

Answer: February, April, June, November

circle

A circle is a 2D shape that is completely round. Different parts of a circle have special names.

circle

see also centre

➤ circular
Circular means in the shape of a circle.

WORD BUILD

➤ arc
An arc is part of the circumference of a circle or any curve. You can draw arcs with compasses.

see also curve

➤ chord
A chord is a straight line that joins two points on the circumference of a circle.

➤ circumference
Circumference is the distance all the way around a circle. It is the perimeter of a circle.

see also perimeter

➤ diameter
Any straight line from one side of a circle to the other is called a diameter. It must go through the centre.

see also centre

➤ quadrant
A quadrant is one quarter of a circle. The straight sides of the quadrant are both radii of the circle.

see also quarter

➤ radius (*plural* radii)
A radius is any straight line from the centre of a circle to the circumference. »

➤ sector
A sector is a slice taken out of a circle. The two straight edges are both radii of the circle and the curved side is an arc. Quadrants and semicircles are types of sector.

➤ segment
A segment is part of a circle. A chord cuts a circle into two segments.

➤ semicircle
A semicircle is half of a circle. The straight side is a diameter of the circle.

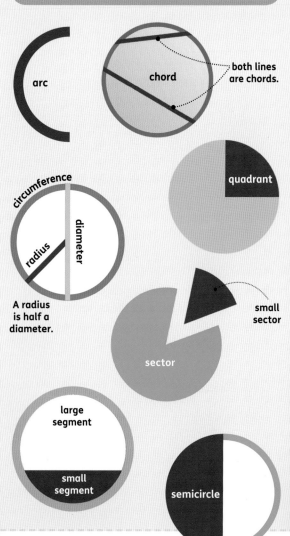

arc — chord — both lines are chords. — circumference — radius — diameter — A radius is half a diameter. — quadrant — small sector — sector — large segment — small segment — semicircle

circumference *see* circle

classify

To classify data is to put data into groups or sets so it can be sorted and interpreted.

EXAMPLE

To find out about journeys to school, the data could be **classified** into the types of transport used.

How children come to school	Number of children
bus	7
car	7
cycle	6
walk	10

class interval

A class interval is a range of numbers or values. You sometimes use class intervals when you are collecting information.

EXAMPLE

Children's pocket money in Pine Hill School

Class interval	Frequency
£0.00 to £0.99	7
£1.00 to £1.99	7
£2.00 to £2.99	9
£3.00 to £3.99	18
£4.00 to £4.99	14
£5.00 or more	4

Somebody who had £4.50 pocket money would be in the **class interval** £4.00 to £4.99.

see also frequency

clockwise

Clockwise means turning the same way as the hands of a clock.

OPPOSITE The opposite of clockwise is anticlockwise.

clockwise

see also anticlockwise, rotate

coin

A coin is money made from metal. Money is also made from paper and called notes. Coins are usually worth less than notes.

column

A column of numbers is written vertically.

A column

1	2	3	4
5	6	7	8
9	10	11	12
13	14	15	16

see also row, vertical

A B **C** D E F G H I J K L M N O P Q R S T U V W X Y Z

column graph *see* graph

common denominator

A common denominator is a multiple of the denominators of two or more fractions. Changing fractions to a common denominator allows you to compare, add and subtract the fractions.

> **EXAMPLE**
>
> 12 is the **common denominator** of thirds and quarters.
>
> Both $\frac{2}{3}$ and $\frac{3}{4}$ can be changed to twelfths.
>
> $\frac{2}{3} = \frac{8}{12}$ $\frac{3}{4} = \frac{9}{12}$

see also denominator, multiple, numerator, lowest common multiple

common factor

A common factor is a number which is a factor of two or more numbers.

> **EXAMPLE**
>
> These are the factors of 12 and 20.
>
> 12: 1 2 3 4 6 12
>
> 20: 1 2 4 5 10 20
>
> The **common factors** of 12 and 20 are 1, 2 and 4.

see also common multiple, factor, lowest common multiple

common fraction *see* fraction

common multiple

Common multiples are any multiples of two or more numbers that are the same.

> **EXAMPLE**
>
> Multiples of 4 include: 4 8 12 16 20 24 ...
>
> Multiples of 6 include: 6 12 18 24 30 ...
>
> The first 2 **common multiples** of 4 and 6 include 12 and 24.
>
> What is the third **common multiple** of 4 and 6?
>
> Answer: 36

see also multiple, lowest common multiple

commutative law

The commutative law of arithmetic says that you can change the order of the numbers when adding or multiplying and the answer will not change. Knowing this property can help make calculations, especially mental calculations, easier.

➤ **commutativity**
Commutativity is the property of being commutative.

> **EXAMPLE**
>
> Addition and multiplication are both **commutative**, but subtraction and division are not.
>
> $6 + 3 + 4 = 6 + 4 + 3$
>
> $2 \times 6 \times 5 = 2 \times 5 \times 6$
>
> $7 - 3 \neq 3 - 7$
>
> $12 \div 4 \neq 4 \div 12$

see also associative law, distributive law

compare

1 To compare things is to see in what ways they are similar or different. Numbers can be compared in different ways. For example, you could find out how much more one number is than another.

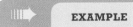

EXAMPLE

Compare 20 and 2,000.

How many times greater is one than the other?

Answer: 100

2 Comparing things is important in measurement. You may need to compare two items to find the heaviest or longest and by how much.

Compare these two lengths:

A

B

How many mm longer is one than the other?

➤ comparison

Comparison is when you see in what ways things are similar or different.

compass

A compass is an instrument used to find direction. The needle on a compass always points to the north.

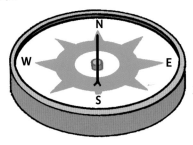

➤ compass points

There are four main compass points, called North, South, East and West. These are called the cardinal points of a compass.

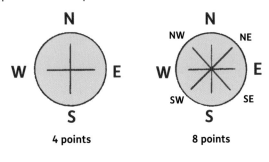

4 points   8 points

There are compass points between N, S, E, and W such as NE, SW, NNE, WSW.

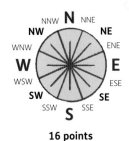

16 points

see also bearing

compasses

Compasses are instruments used to draw circles or arcs.

see also circle

compass points *see* compass

a
b
c
d
e
f
g
h
i
j
k
l
m
n
o
p
q
r
s
t
u
v
w
x
y
z

complement

A complement is what is needed to make something complete.

> **EXAMPLE**
>
> 30 and 70 are **complements** of 100.
>
> 20° and 70° are **complements** of a right angle. $\frac{1}{4}$ and $\frac{3}{4}$ are **complements** of 1.

composite number *see* number

composite shape

A composite shape is a 2D shape made from a number of other 2D shapes. The area of composite shapes is often found by breaking up the shape into its composite rectangles or triangles.

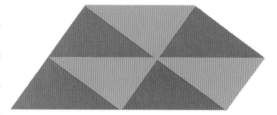

see also rectilinear shape

concave

Concave means curved inwards like a cave.

OPPOSITE The opposite of concave is convex.

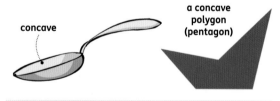

concave

a concave polygon (pentagon)

see also convex

concentric

Shapes that are concentric have a centre that is in common. A bullseye target is made up of concentric circles.

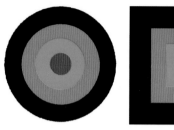 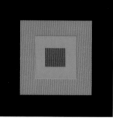

concentric circles   concentric squares

see also centre

concrete objects

Concrete objects in mathematics are any items that can be picked up and manipulated to help understand a concept or idea.

Cubes are concrete objects used to help understand basic arithmetic.

cone

A cone has a flat base that is a circle. The top comes to a point and its sides are curved.

see also apex, base

➤ **conical**

A conical shape is one that looks like a cone.

cone

conical shapes

congruent

Two shapes are congruent if they are exactly the same. They can be in different positions, but must have sides, lengths and angles that are identical.

construct

When you construct a shape you draw it very accurately using instruments such as a ruler, compasses, protractor and set square.

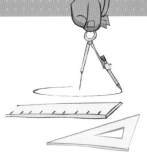

You should use a sharp pencil when constructing.

continuous data *see* data

consecutive

Consecutive means one after the other in a regular order.

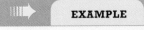

> **EXAMPLE**

14, 15, 16, 17 are **consecutive** whole numbers.

7, 9, 11, 13 are **consecutive** odd numbers.

1, 4, 9, 16 are **consecutive** square numbers.

convert

When you convert something you change it from one thing into another.

➤ conversion

Conversion is when you change something from one thing into another. You can use conversion graphs and tables when converting between units.

> **EXAMPLE**

120 cm **converts** into 1.2 metres.

5°C **converts** into 41°F.

constant

A constant is a value that stays the same when it is used in an equation.

> **EXAMPLE**

$a = 3 + y$

The 3 is a **constant** in this equation.
The a and y are both variables.

see also variable

convex

Convex means curved outwards.

OPPOSITE The opposite of convex is concave.

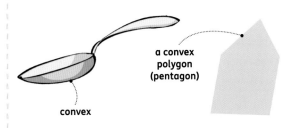

a convex polygon (pentagon)

convex

see also concave

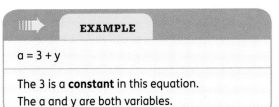

coordinate

Coordinates are two numbers or letters that describe a position on maps, graphs and charts. The horizontal coordinate is always written first and the vertical coordinate is always written second.

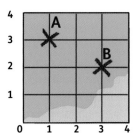

The coordinates of A are (1,3).
The x-coordinate is 1.
The y-coordinate is 3.

The coordinates of B are (3,2).
The x-coordinate is 3.
The y-coordinate is 2.

○ x-coordinate

The x-coordinate is the horizontal distance from the origin where the two axes meet. It is the first number in the number pair.

○ y-coordinate

The y-coordinate is the vertical distance from the origin where the two axes meet. It is the second number in the number pair.

see also axis, origin

correct

❶ When something is correct it is accurate, proper or right.
OPPOSITE The opposite of correct is incorrect.
❷ If you correct something you make it right by removing the error.

➤ **correction**

A correction is what you do to make a mistake right.

EXAMPLE
3 × 4 = ?
The **correct** answer is 12.
error 3 × 4 = 14
correction 3 × 4 = 12

correspondence problem

Solving a correspondence problem involves multiplying or dividing numbers of different objects that at have a given relationship between them.

EXAMPLE
'Super socks' are sold in packs with 2 stripy pairs and 3 spotty pairs of stocks. Danny buys some packs and has 8 pairs of stripy socks. How many pairs of spotty socks does he have?

Answer: 12 pairs

cost price

Cost price is what a person pays to buy something. A manufacturer's selling price is a shopkeeper's cost price. The shopkeeper adds on a profit and sells it to a customer.

EXAMPLE
A shopkeeper buys an item for $75 (**cost price**).
The shopkeeper sells the item for $100 (selling price).
The shopkeeper's selling price is the customer's **cost price**.

see also loss, profit

cross-section

A cross-section is a cut straight through a 3D shape. It is a slice of an object.

a cross-section of a tooth

The cross-section of a cylinder is a circle.

see also cylinder

cube

❶ A cube is a 3D shape with six square faces.
A cube has six faces, eight vertices and 12 edges.

All these are cubes.

❷ The cube of a number is the number multiplied by itself twice. The cube of four is $4 \times 4 \times 4$.

➤ **cubed**

When a number is cubed it is multiplied by itself twice.

> **EXAMPLE**
>
> Seven **cubed** is $7 \times 7 \times 7$ which is written as 7^3.

see also cube root, square, square root, index

cube root

The cube root of a number is that number which, multiplied by itself twice, gives the number to be cube rooted. The symbol for cube root is $\sqrt[3]{}$.

> **EXAMPLE**
>
> The **cube root** of 27 is 3 because $3 \times 3 \times 3 = 27$.
>
> The **cube root** of 27 is written as $\sqrt[3]{27}$.
>
> The **cube root** of 125 is 5 because $5 \times 5 \times 5 = 125$.
>
> The **cube root** of 125 is written as $\sqrt[3]{125}$.

see also cube, square, square root, index

cubic centimetre (*also* cm³)

A cubic centimetre is used as a measure for the volume of containers or objects. A cubic centimetre is the space taken up by a 1 cm cube. The short way of writing cubic centimetre is cm³.

Volume = 8 cubic centimetres or 8 cm³.

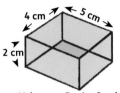

Volume = 5 × 4 × 2 cubic centimetres or 40 cm³.

see also cubic metre, volume

cubic metre (*also* m³)

A cubic metre is used as a measure for the volume of quite large containers or objects. A cubic metre is the space taken up by a 1 metre cube. The short way of writing cubic metre is m³.

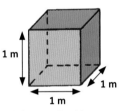

Volume = 1 cubic metre or 1 m³.

see also cubic centimetre, volume

cubit

A cubit is the distance from the tip of the middle finger to the elbow. The Ancient Egyptian Royal Cubit was made from granite and subdivided into seven palms each of four digits. It was one of the very first standard units of measurement but it is not used today.

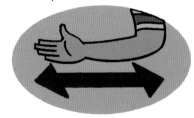

cubit

see also palm, standard unit

cuboid

A cuboid is a 3D shape shaped like a box, with six rectangular faces. A cuboid has six faces, eight vertices and 12 edges.

These are all cuboids.

Some cuboids have one pair of square faces.

see also cube, face, rectangle, square

currency

Currency is the money that is used in a country.

> **EXAMPLE**
>
> The **currency** used in the UK is the pound.
>
> The **currency** used in the USA is the dollar.

see also denomination, exchange rate

curve

A curve is a bend. Curves can be lines or surfaces.

a curved line

A cone has a curved surface.

see also arc, edge, line, surface

cylinder

A cylinder is a 3D shape shaped like a roller. It has two flat faces and one curved surface. Cross-sections of a cylinder, parallel to the base, or its flat faces, are all identically sized circles.

see also cross-section, face

➤ cylindrical

A cylindrical object is one shaped like a cylinder.

Cylindrical shapes are shaped like cylinders.

Dd

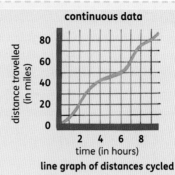

continuous data

line graph of distances cycled

D

The Romans used the letter D to stand for the number 500.

EXAMPLE

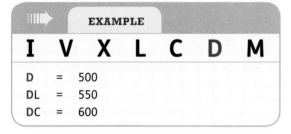

I	V	X	L	C	D	M

D	=	500
DL	=	550
DC	=	600

see also Roman numerals

data

Data is information or facts that you are given or that you find out. Data can be words, numbers or a mixture of both. Mathematical data and measurements are often presented in tables, graphs and charts.

see also database, statistics, graph, chart, classify

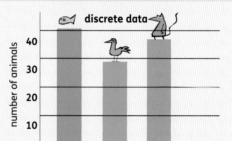

discrete data

number of animals

fish   birds   mice

animals in a pet shop

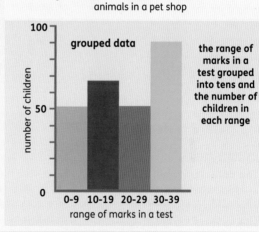

grouped data

number of children

0-9 10-19 20-29 30-39

range of marks in a test

the range of marks in a test grouped into tens and the number of children in each range

○ continuous data

Continuous data is data that can be measured at any point on a scale. It is often shown using a line graph.

see also graph

○ discrete data

Discrete data is data that can be counted. It is shown in distinct, separated groups, such as in bar charts.

see also chart

○ grouped data

Sometimes data is grouped together in blocks like these times:

2:30 to 2:59

3:00 to 3:29

3:30 to 3:59

The times between 2:30 and 4:00 are grouped together in half hour blocks.

The class interval of the grouped data is half an hour.

see also class interval

database

A database is a large amount of information often stored in a computer. You can use the database to sort the information in different ways.

> **EXAMPLE**
>
> Bookshops use a **database** to store information about the books:
>
> • author
>
> • publisher
>
> • publication date
>
> • price
>
> • reference number

date

Dates can be used to tell you when something happened or will happen. Usually a date tells you the day, month and year. History dates often only use the year.

> **EXAMPLE**
>
> 25th May 1943
> This **date** shows day, month and year.
>
> 16.04.20
> This **date** is the 16th of April in the year 2020.
>
> William Shakespeare 1564–1616
> This **date** shows the years in which Shakespeare was born and died.

see also calendar

day

A day is one-seventh of a week and lasts for 24 hours. Each day starts at midnight.

> **EXAMPLE**
>
> The seven **days** in a week are Sunday, Monday, Tuesday, Wednesday, Thursday, Friday and Saturday.

deca-

Deca- is used as a prefix to show the number 10.

> **EXAMPLE**
>
> A **deca**gon is a polygon with 10 sides.

decade

A decade is a period of 10 years.

> **EXAMPLE**
>
> The year 2019 is at the end of the **decade** which runs from 1st January 2010 to 31st December 2019.

see also year, century

decagon

A decagon is any 2D shape that has 10 straight sides. If all the sides and angles are the same size it is a regular decagon.

a regular decagon

see also polygon

decahedron (*plural* decahedra)

A decahedron is any 3D shape that has 10 flat faces. Deca- at the start of a word often means 'ten'.

An octagonal prism is an example of a decahedron.

see also polyhedron

decilitre (*also* dl)

A decilitre is one tenth of a litre.
There are 100 millilitres in 1 decilitre.
Deci- at the start of a word usually means 'one tenth'.

> **EXAMPLE**
>
> 10 **decilitres** = 1 litre
> 10 **dl** = 1 l
> 1 **dl** = $\frac{1}{10}$ litre
> ---
> 1 litre = 100 centilitres
> 1 **dl** = 10 cl
> ---
> 1 litre = 1,000 millilitres
> 1 **dl** = 100 ml

see also centilitre, litre, millilitre

decimal comma
see decimal number

decimal fraction
see decimal number

decimal number

You use decimal numbers (or decimal notation) when you use hundreds, tens and ones. Decimals are based on ten, multiples of ten and tenths. A decimal point separates whole numbers from decimal fractions.

> **EXAMPLE**
>
> 124.75
> ---
> This **decimal number** is made up of:
> ---
> | 1 hundred | 7 tenths |
> | 2 tens | 5 hundredths |
> | 4 ones | |

see also digit, place value

➤ decimal comma

In many countries (such as France, Indonesia and South Africa) the decimal comma is used to separate whole numbers from the fractions in a decimal number. In these countries, the decimal comma is used in the same way as the decimal point. In this book the decimal point has been used throughout.

> **EXAMPLE**
>
> €5,50
> This means 5 euros and 50 cents.
> ---
> R70,00
> This means 70 South African rand.

➤ decimal fraction

A decimal fraction is a sort of fraction that uses tenths, hundredths, thousandths and so on. Decimal fractions represent the digits to the right of the decimal point.

> **EXAMPLE**
>
> $0.5 = \frac{5}{10} = \frac{1}{2}$
> ---
> $0.25 = \frac{25}{100} = \frac{1}{4}$
> ---
> $0.125 = \frac{125}{1,000} = \frac{1}{8}$
> ---
> We use the decimal point to create **decimal fractions**.

see also place value, recurring decimal

a b c d e f g h i j k l m n o p q r s t u v w x y z

➤ decimal place

Decimal place is the number of digits after the decimal point. You sometimes have to write numbers to a certain number of decimal places.

EXAMPLE

12.56 has 2 **decimal places**.
0.228 has 3 **decimal places**.
0.00675 has 5 **decimal places**.
3.234677 written to 2 **decimal places** is 3.23

see also digit, round

➤ decimal point

❶ A decimal point is used to separate the whole numbers from the fractions in a decimal number. It comes between the digit for the ones and the digit for the tenths.

❷ The decimal point is used in many countries (such as the UK and the US) and is also used by all technology (such as calculators and computers). In this book the decimal point has been used throughout.

EXAMPLE

42.6 This number says forty-two **point** six.
6.64 m Measurements also use the **decimal point**.

decimal place
see decimal number

decimal point
see decimal number

decimetre (*also* dm)

A decimetre is one tenth of a metre. There are 10 centimetres in one decimetre. Deci- at the start of a word usually means 'one tenth'. The short way of writing decimetre is dm.

EXAMPLE

10 **decimetres** = 1 metre
10 **dm** = 10 m
1 **decimetre** = 10 centimetres
1 **dm** = 10 cm
1 **decimetre** = 0.1 metre

see also **centimetre**

decrease

When you decrease something you make it less or smaller.

EXAMPLE

Decrease 65 by 15.
Decrease 5 by 2.

Answers: 65 − 15 = 50   5 − 2 = 3

5 − 2 = 3
5 decreased
by 2 equals 3.

see also subtraction

deep

Deep is how far down or back something goes. For example, water can be deep and so can a cave.

see also breadth, depth, shallow, width

degree

❶ Degree (°) is a unit used to measure the size of angles. A complete turn measures 360°.

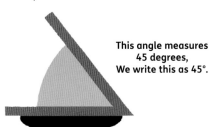

This angle measures 45 degrees,
We write this as 45°.

❷ Degree is a unit used to measure temperature. There are different types of degrees. The most common are degrees Celsius (°C) and degrees Fahrenheit (°F).

EXAMPLE
Using **degrees** Celsius: Water boils at 100°C and freezes at 0°C.
Using **degrees** Fahrenheit: Water boils at 212°F and freezes at 32°F.

see also angle, bearing

denomination

The denomination of a particular note or coin is its value as part of the currency of a country.

see also currency

denominator

The bottom number of a fraction is called the denominator. The denominator tells you how many equal parts the quantity or shape has been divided into.

	EXAMPLE
$\frac{3}{4}$	3 is the numerator.
	4 is the **denominator**.

see also common denominator, fraction, numerator

depth

Depth is a measure of deepness. It is the distance down or back.

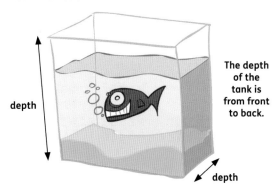

The depth of the tank is from front to back.

depth

depth

The depth of the water is from the surface to the bottom.

see also breadth, deep, height, width

a b c d e f g h i j k l m n o p q r s t u v w x y z

descending

Descending means going down or reducing in size.

OPPOSITE The opposite of descending is ascending.

➡	**EXAMPLE**

74   66   42   30   23

These numbers are in **descending** order.

see also ascending

diagonal

A diagonal is a straight line that joins any two corners which are not adjacent.

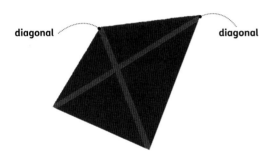

diagonal   diagonal

Diagonals do not always cut a shape in half or go through the middle.

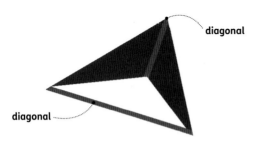

diagonal

diagonal

A diagonal can be outside the shape.

see also circle

diagram

A diagram is a drawing or picture used to make something clear or simple.

This diagram shows two types of cyinder.

see also plan

⚙ Carroll diagram

A Carroll diagram is used for sorting. One part of the diagram is the opposite of the other. Carroll diagrams are named after the author, Lewis Carroll.

⚙ flow diagram

A flow diagram is a useful way of showing an operation or series of operations that must be performed on a number or set of numbers.

see also input value, output value

⚙ tree diagram

A tree diagram can be used for sorting. When using a tree diagram you often have to make a YES or NO choice.

⚙ Venn diagram

A Venn diagram is used for sorting sets of things.

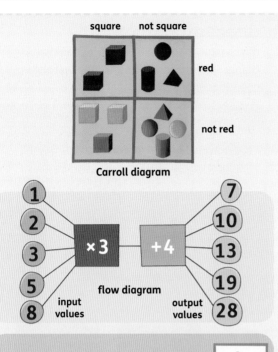

Carroll diagram

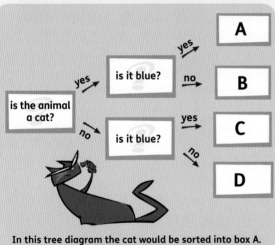

flow diagram

input values
output values

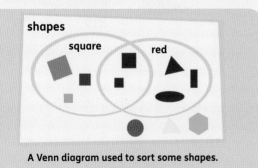

In this tree diagram the cat would be sorted into box A.

tree diagram

shapes

A Venn diagram used to sort some shapes.

Venn diagram

diameter see circle

diamond

A diamond is another name for a rhombus.
It is a four-sided shape without right angles.
All four sides are the same length.

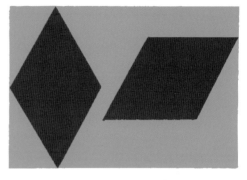

see also polygon, quadrilateral, rhombus

difference

The difference between two numbers is the value of how much one is greater than the other.
It can found by subtracting the smallest number from the largest, or by counting on from the smallest to the largest.

The difference between 5 and 2 is 3.
5 − 2 = 3

see also subtraction

digit

There are ten digits. They are 0, 1, 2, 3, 4, 5, 6, 7, 8 and 9. These digits are used to build up other numbers.

⏩ EXAMPLE
27 is a 2-**digit** number.
235 is a 3-**digit** number.
1,067 is a 4-**digit** number.

see also place value

digital clock

A digital clock or watch has only numbers on it instead of a dial and hands.

Analogue clocks have hands.

Digital clock have numbers only.

see also analogue clock

dimension

Dimensions are measurements of size such as length, width, height and radius.

A line has one dimension, length.

A plane shape has two dimensions, length and width.

A solid shape has three dimensions, length, width and height.

see also two-dimensional shape, three-dimensional shape

direct proportion

If a change in one quantity causes a similar change in another quantity, we say that the quantities are in direct proportion.

⏩ EXAMPLE
If chocolates cost $2.00 each and you buy 10, the total cost is $20.00
However, if you buy 15 chocolates the total cost is $30.00—as the number of chocolates increases so does the total cost.
The number of chocolates and the total cost are in **direct proportion**.

$2.00 **$20.00** **$30.00**

see also indirect proportion

discount

A discount is a reduction in the cost of something. You often get a discount for paying early or buying in large quantities.

FULL PRICE £200
DISCOUNT PRICE £175
YOU SAVE £25

FULL PRICE R100
DISCOUNT PRICE R90
YOU SAVE R10

see also decrease, per cent, reduction

discrete data *see* data

distance

Distance tells you how far apart two things are. The shortest distance between two places is a straight line. Distances are measured in units such as centimetres, metres and kilometres.

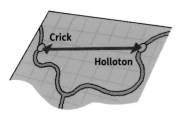

The distance between the towns by road is greater than the distance in a straight line.

distributive law

The distributive law explains how multiplication and addition can be used together in a certain way. Multiplying by a number formed by adding two or more numbers gives the same answer as doing each multiplication separately with those numbers.

EXAMPLE
$a \times (b + c) = (a \times b) + (a \times c)$
So $4 \times (5 + 2) = (4 \times 5) + (4 \times 2)$.
This shows that 4×7 can be worked out as follows: • Break up the 7 into $5 + 2$. • Multiply both numbers by 4.

see also associative law, commutative law

divide

When you divide you share things equally or group a quantity into a number of equal parts. To divide a number by another number is to find out how many times the second number is contained in the first. The symbol for 'divided by' is ÷.

8 divided by 4 equals 2 groups.

$8 ÷ 4 = 2$

see also division, remainder, share

dividend

❶ When you divide one number into another, the dividend is the number that has to be divided.

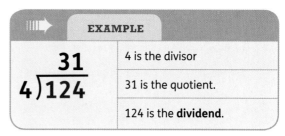

EXAMPLE	
$\dfrac{31}{4\overline{)124}}$	4 is the divisor
	31 is the quotient.
	124 is the **dividend**.

see also divisor, quotient

❷ A dividend is what you receive as interest on money you have invested.

EXAMPLE
Invest £100 Receive a **dividend** of 5p for each £1. Total £105
Invest R100 Receive a **dividend** of 5c for each R1. Total R105

see also interest

divisibility rules

Divisibility rules are quick checks to see whether one number will divide exactly into another.

EXAMPLE
Some **divisibility rules**:
All even numbers are **divisible** by 2.
All whole numbers that end in 5 or 0 are **divisible** by 5.

see also dividend, divisor, quotient, divide

divisible

One number is divisible by another number if the remainder is zero.

> **EXAMPLE**
>
> $45 \div 9 = 5$
> 45 is **divisible** by 9 because there is no remainder.
>
> $48 \div 9 = 5 \text{ r}3$
> 48 is not **divisible** by 9 because there is a remainder.

see also dividend, divisor, quotient, remainder, divide

division

❶ Division is sharing things.
❷ Division is grouping into sets of the same size.
The symbol for division is ÷.

> **EXAMPLE**
>
> **Division** by sharing things equally:
>
> What is 8 divided by 2?
> $8 \div 2 = 4$
>
> **Division** by grouping into sets of the same size:
>
> How many twos are in 8?
> $8 \div 2 = 4$

8 shared between 2 is 4 each.

8 in groups of 2 gives 4 groups.

see also dividend, divisor, quotient, remainder, share

divisor

When you divide one number into another, the divisor is the number that is divided into the other.

> **EXAMPLE**
>
>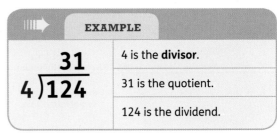
>
> | | |
> |---|---|
> | | 4 is the **divisor**. |
> | | 31 is the quotient. |
> | | 124 is the dividend. |

see also dividend, divisor, quotient, divide

dodecagon

A dodecagon is any 2D shape that has 12 straight sides. A regular dodecagon has all its sides and angles equal.

a regular dodecagon

dodecahedron

(*plural* dodecahedra)

A dodecahedron is a 3D shape that has 12 flat faces. A regular dodecahedron has 12 pentagon faces.

a regular dodecahedron

see also polyhedron, pentagon

double

Double is twice as many.

> **EXAMPLE**
>
> **Double** 15 is 30.

see also treble, triple

duration

The duration of an event is the amount of time from start to finish.

Ee

edge

The edge of a shape is where two faces meet. An edge can be straight or curved.

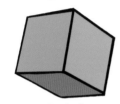

A cube has
12 straight edges.

A cylinder has
2 curved edges.

see also face, vertex,
three-dimensional shape

ellipse

An ellipse is like a flattened circle. It has two lines of symmetry.

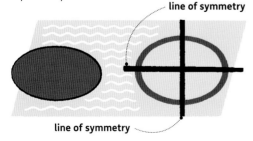

line of symmetry

line of symmetry

empty set *see* set

enlarge

If you enlarge something you make it bigger.

OPPOSITE The opposite of enlarge is reduce.

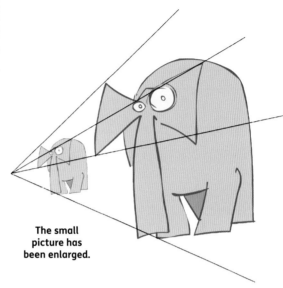

The small
picture has
been enlarged.

see also reduce, scale

equal

Two things are equal if they are the same in some way. Numbers or calculations are equal when they are worth the same. The symbol for equal to is $=$.

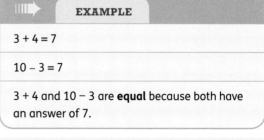

A

B

The rods are equal in length but have different thickness and colour.

▐▐▐▶	**EXAMPLE**
$3 + 4 = 7$	
$10 - 3 = 7$	
$3 + 4$ and $10 - 3$ are **equal** because both have an answer of 7.	

see also equal sign, equivalent, unequal

a
b
c
d
e
f
g
h
i
j
k
l
m
n
o
p
q
r
s
t
u
v
w
x
y
z

equal sign

The equal sign or the symbol **=** is used to show equal quantities or numbers. It was first used by Robert Recorde in 1557.

> **EXAMPLE**
>
> $3 \times 4 = 12$
>
> $100 \text{ cm} = 1 \text{ metre}$
>
> $3 + y = 10$

see also equation

equation

An equation has two parts separated by an equal sign. The left part of an equation is always worth the same as the right part.

> **EXAMPLE**
>
> Here are some **equations**:
>
> $5 + [\ ] = 9$
> $5 + 4 = 9$
>
> $12 - y = 3$
> $12 - 9 = 3$
>
> $2b + 4 = b + 7$
> $6 + 4 = 3 + 7$

see also equal sign

equilateral triangle
see **triangle**

equivalent

Equivalent means worth the same. Equivalent things may look different but they always have the same value.

>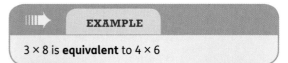
>
> **EXAMPLE**
>
> 3×8 is **equivalent** to 4×6

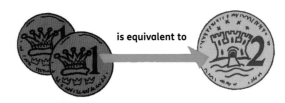

is equivalent to

see also equal

equivalent fraction see fraction

equivalent ratio see ratio

Eratosthenes sieve

Eratosthenes was a Greek mathematician who lived between 275 and 195 BC. He found a way of finding prime numbers using a method called the Sieve of Eratosthenes or Eratosthenes sieve.

> **EXAMPLE**
>
> To find prime numbers up to 100 using the **Eratosthenes sieve**.
>
> Cross out 1.
>
> Cross out multiples of 2 but not 2.
>
> Cross out multiples of 3 but not 3.
>
> Cross out multiples of 5 but not 5.
>
> Cross out multiples of 7 but not 7.
>
> The numbers not crossed out are prime numbers.

see also number

estimate

When you make an estimate you judge the amount without measuring or calculation. A guess is different to an estimate. When you guess you do not have any idea of the answer.

➤ **estimation**

Estimation is judging an amount without measuring or calculation.

What is your estimation of the length of this line in cm?

Answer: between 10 cm and 14 cm is a good estimate

see also guess

evening

Evening comes after the afternoon. It is the end of the daytime. We often talk about early evening and late evening.

9:00 p.m.

nine o'clock in the evening

see also afternoon, morning

even number *see* number

event

An event is something that can happen when we perform an experiment. When we toss a coin there are two possible events. When we roll a dice there are many different possible events.

> **EXAMPLE**
>
> Rolling a dice may give us any one of these different **events**:
>
> | | |
> |---|---|
> | 2 4 6 | an even number |
> | 1 3 5 | an odd number |
> | 2 3 5 | a prime number |
> | 3 6 | a number divisible by 3 |

exact

When something is exact it is neither more nor less.

➤ **exactly**

When you measure exactly you measure very accurately.

The rods are exactly the same length.

see also accurate

exchange

When you exchange something you change it for something else. Usually the things you exchange are worth the same.

The money can be exchanged for the stamp.

exchange rate

The exchange rate is the value of a currency when it is exchanged to the currency of another country.

 EXAMPLE

The **exchange rate** for £ (pounds sterling) to € (Euro) is approximately £1 = €1.20

see also currency

exponent

Exponent is the name we give to the number 2 in the expression: 5^2. We say the exponent of 5 is 2. This is also known as an index.

 **EXAMPLE**

$5^2 = 5 \times 5$

see also squared, index, power

exterior angle see angle

face

A face is the side of a solid shape. It usually means flat faces. The base of a shape is also a face.

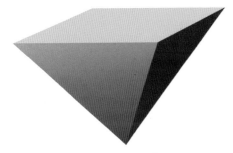

This pyramid has 5 faces.

see also base, edge, vertex

factor

A factor is a whole number that will divide exactly into another number.

> **EXAMPLE**
>
> 3 is a **factor** of 21.
>
> 7 is a **factor** of 63.
>
> 2 and 7 are both **factors** of 14.

see also divisor, multiple, factor pair, common factor, highest common factor, prime factor

factorise (*also* factorize)

To factorise a number is to write that number as the product of its factors. This is helpful for carrying out mental calculations.

> **EXAMPLE**
>
> 18 could be **factorised** into 6×3 or $2 \times 3 \times 3$.
>
> To work out 5×18 mentally you could **factorise** 18:
> $5 \times 6 \times 3 = 30 \times 3 = 90$.

see also factor, product

factor pair

A factor pair are two numbers that give a particular product when multiplied together.

> **EXAMPLE**
>
> The **factor pairs** of 12 are:
>
> | 1 and 12 | 2 and 6 | 3 and 4 |
> |---|---|---|

see also factor, product

Fahrenheit (*also* °F)

Fahrenheit is a scale that is sometimes used for measuring temperature. It is written as degrees Fahrenheit (°F). It is named after the German scientist G.D. Fahrenheit.

> **EXAMPLE**
>
> Using the **Fahrenheit** scale, the freezing point of water is 32°**F** and the boiling point is 212°**F**.

see also Celsius, centigrade

fathom

A fathom is a standard unit of six feet (1.83 m). Originally a fathom was the distance between the fingertips of a sailor's outstretched arms. It was used to measure the depths of oceans.

Sailors used a weighted rope marked with fathoms.

see also cubit

Fibonacci sequence

The Fibonacci sequence is named after Leonardo Fibonacci, a 13th century Italian mathematician. It is a sequence of numbers where each number is found by adding the two previous numbers.

> **EXAMPLE**
>
> The best known **Fibonacci sequence** begins with
>
> 1 1 2 3 5 8 13 21 34
>
> What do you think the next number will be in the sequence?
>
> Answer: 55

see also sequence

figure

A figure is a number used to write an integer.

> **EXAMPLE**
>
> The number twenty six in **figures** is 26.

see also digit, number, numeral

flat

Flat means smooth and level.

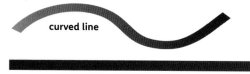

curved line

flat line

see also curve, edge, face

flat angle *see* angle

flat shape

A flat shape is very thin. 2D shapes are sometimes called flat shapes.

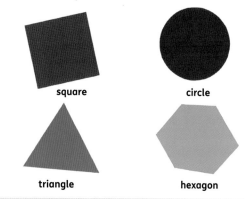

square   circle

triangle   hexagon

see also two-dimensional shape

flip

To flip a shape is to turn it over.

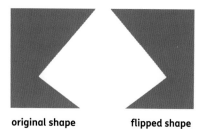

original shape   flipped shape

see also reflect, transformation

flow diagram *see* diagram

foot (*plural* feet)

A foot is an imperial unit used to measure length.
A foot is divided into 12 equal parts called inches.
A foot measures about 30 cm.

⇨ EXAMPLE
1 **foot** = 12 inches
3 **feet** = 1 yard
1 **foot** = 30.48 cm

see also metric units

formula (*plural* formulae)

A formula is a rule that tells you how to work
something out based on certain values. A formula
can be given in words or using letters and symbols.

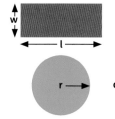

Formula for finding the
area of a rectangle:
$a = l \times w$

Formula for finding the
circumference of a circle:
$c = 2 \times \pi \times r$

see also equation

fraction

Fractions are usually parts of something.
The bottom part of a fraction is called the
denominator. It tells you the number of equal
parts. The top part is the numerator. It tells you
the number of those parts you are dealing with.

The circle has
been divided into
four equal parts.

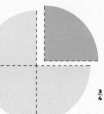

Three parts
are light blue
and one part is
darker blue.

$\frac{3}{4}$ is light blue
and $\frac{1}{4}$ is
darker blue.

see also denominator, numerator

WORD BUILD

➤ fraction as a quotient

A quotient is the result of dividing two
numbers. When a larger number is divided
into a smaller number the quotient is a
fraction. When one number is not exactly
divisible by another the quotient can be
written as a mixed number.

$3 \div 4 = \frac{3}{4}$

When you divide 3 by 4 the **quotient** is the
fraction $\frac{3}{4}$.

$15 \div 4 = 3\frac{3}{4}$

When you divide 15 by 4 the **quotient** is the
mixed number $3\frac{3}{4}$.

see also number, quotient

➤ fraction as a ratio

A fraction can be a ratio between two
numbers. Two out of three apples were
bad.

The fraction of bad apples was $\frac{2}{3}$.

see also proportion, ratio

➤ fraction of a quantity

When you find the **fraction of a quantity** you
divide by the denominator and multiply by
the numerator.

$\frac{1}{5}$ of 20 = 4.

$\frac{1}{4}$ of 12 = 3.

$\frac{4}{5}$ of 20 = 16.

$\frac{3}{4}$ of 12 = 9.

see also division

common fraction

A common fraction is a fraction written in the form of a number above another number, separated by a bar. A common fraction is also known as a vulgar fraction.

$\frac{1}{2}$ $\frac{3}{5}$ $\frac{13}{20}$ are all **common fractions**.

decimal fraction
see decimal number

equivalent fraction

Equivalent fractions are worth the same. When you simplify a fraction the new fraction is equivalent to the original fraction.

see also cancel, simplify

improper fraction

An improper fraction has a numerator larger than its denominator. It is a fraction that is worth more than one.

$\frac{7}{3}$ is an **improper fraction**.

see also number

like fractions

Like fractions are fractions that all have the same denominator.

$\frac{1}{8}$ $\frac{3}{8}$ $\frac{5}{8}$ $\frac{7}{8}$ are all **like fractions**.

non-unit fraction

A non-unit fraction is any common fraction with a numerator that is greater than 1. Each **non-unit fraction** shows more than one part of a whole divided into equal parts.

proper fraction

A proper fraction is when the numerator is smaller than the denominator. It is a fraction worth less than 1.

$\frac{7}{8}$ is a **proper fraction**.

top-heavy fraction

A top-heavy fraction has the numerator larger than the denominator. It is an improper fraction. All top-heavy fractions are greater than 1. All top-heavy fractions can be changed to mixed numbers.

$\frac{7}{3} = 2\frac{1}{3}$

$\frac{7}{3}$ is the **top-heavy fraction** that can be changed to the mixed number of $2\frac{1}{3}$.

see also mixed number

unit fraction

A unit fraction has any number as the denominator and a 1 as the numerator. The denominator shows how many the whole is divided into.

$\frac{1}{3}$ $\frac{1}{8}$ $\frac{1}{100}$ are all **unit fractions**.

see also number

unlike fractions

Unlike fractions are fractions that have different denominators.

$\frac{3}{5}$ and $\frac{2}{3}$ are **unlike** fractions.

vulgar fraction

A vulgar fraction is the same as a common fraction.

$\frac{2}{3}$ is a **vulgar fraction**.

frequency

Frequency is how often something happens.

➤ frequency table

A frequency table is used to record frequency. Tally marks are often used to show the frequency in a frequency table or chart.

MARKS	FREQUENCY	
21-25	III	3
16-20	LHT II	7
11-15	LHT LHT	10
6-10	IIII	4
1-5	LHT	5

The frequency table shows marks scored in a test.

see also tally

function

A function is a rule given to a set of numbers (the input) that changes those numbers (the output). The relationship between input and output numbers is kept the same for any numbers used.

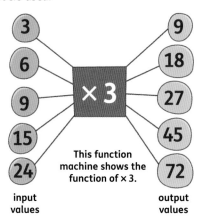

input values

output values

This function machine shows the function of × 3.

gallon

A gallon is an imperial unit used to measure capacity. A gallon is divided into eight parts called pints. A gallon measures about $4\frac{1}{2}$ litres.

➤	EXAMPLE

1 **gallon** = 8 pints

1 **gallon** = 4 quarts

1 **gallon** = 4.55 litres

see also capacity, imperial units, metric units

geometry

Geometry is the part of mathematics that deals with lines, curves, angles and shapes.

➤ geometric (*also* geometrical)

Geometric (or geometrical) means to do with geometry. Geometrical shapes are made from straight lines, circles and arcs.

see also angle, circle

giga-

Giga- is used as a prefix to show the number 1 billion (1,000,000,000)

> **EXAMPLE**
>
> Some computers have 16 **giga**byte of memory

see also mega-

gradient

The gradient of a line drawn on a graph is how steep the line is. It is also called a slope. To calculate the gradient on a line graph, divide the vertical change by the horizontal change.

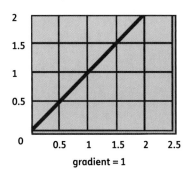

gradient = 1

gram (*also* g)

Grams are metric units of mass used to weigh things. There are 1,000 grams in a kilogram. One gram is very light. The short way of writing gram is g.

> **EXAMPLE**
>
> 1,000 **grams** = 1 kilogram
>
> 1,000 **g** = 1 kg

see also mass, metric units, weight

graph

A graph is a picture, chart or diagram showing information about things.

see also chart, data, pictogram

○ **bar graph** *see* **chart**

○ **bar-line graph**

A bar-line graph is a graph that has lines instead of bars to show information. The lines can be horizontal or vertical.

○ **block graph**

A block graph is a graph made up of blocks. The blocks are usually square.

○ **column graph**

A column graph is a bar chart with each of the bars arranged vertically.

○ **line graph**

A line graph is a type of graph used to show continuous data. Points on the graph are joined with a line to show a trend.

see also data

greater than (*also* more than, larger than)

You use the words 'greater than' when comparing two unequal numbers. You can also use 'more than' or 'larger than'. The symbol for greater than is **>**.

> **EXAMPLE**
>
> ## 12 > 7
>
> 12 is **greater than** 7.

see also equal, less than, symbol

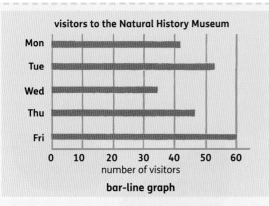

visitors to the Natural History Museum

number of visitors

bar-line graph

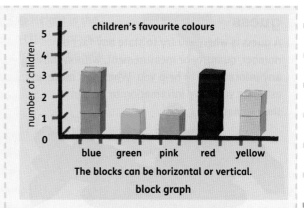

children's favourite colours

number of children

blue green pink red yellow

The blocks can be horizontal or vertical.

block graph

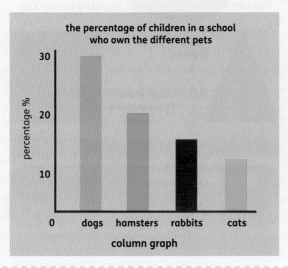

the percentage of children in a school who own the different pets

percentage %

dogs hamsters rabbits cats

column graph

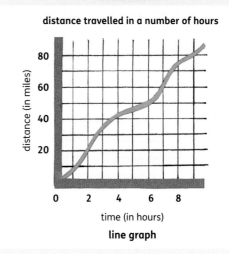

distance travelled in a number of hours

distance (in miles)

time (in hours)

line graph

a b c d e f g h i j k l m n o p q r s t u v w x y z

Greenwich Mean Time (*also* GMT)

Greenwich Mean Time (GMT) is a standard time measured at the Prime Meridian at the Royal Observatory in Greenwich, London.

 EXAMPLE

Greenwich Mean Time (GMT) is the standard local time in the UK in the winter months. In March, this local time is moved forward by one hour to British Summer Time (BST) until the end of October.

see also British Summer Time

grid

A grid is usually two or more sets of parallel lines crossing each other. Most grids are squares but they can be rectangles or triangles.

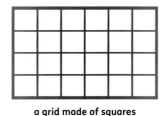

a grid made of squares

grouped data *see* data

hexagon

A hexagon is any polygon that has six straight sides. in a regular hexagon all the sides and angles are equal.

regular hexagon   irregular hexagon

see also polygon, two-dimensional shape

➤ hexagonal

Hexagonal shapes have six sides.

hexagonal prism see prism

hexahedron (*plural* hexahedra)

A hexahedron is any solid shape that has six flat faces.

This hexahedron has
6 triangle faces.

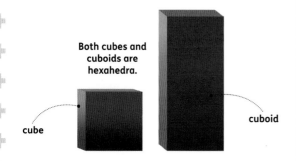

Both cubes and cuboids are hexahedra.

cube   cuboid

see also polyhedron,
three-dimensional shape

hexomino (*plural* hexominoes)

A shape made from arranging six identical squares together is called a hexomino. The squares are joined at their sides.

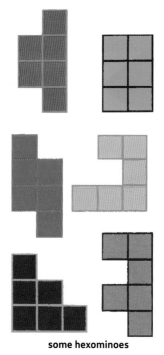

some hexominoes

see also pentomino

highest common factor (*also* HCF)

The highest common factor of a set of numbers is the largest factor of all the numbers in the set. The initials HCF mean highest common factor.

EXAMPLE
8 12 20
Four is the largest number that will divide exactly into all these numbers.
The **highest common factor** of 8, 12 and 20 is 4.
The **HCF** of 8, 12 and 20 is 4.

see also factor, lowest common multiple

histogram

A histogram is similar to a bar chart, with each bar showing grouped data in a specified range. The height of each bar shows how many are in each range.

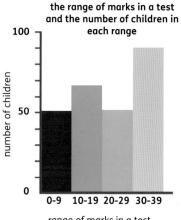

the range of marks in a test and the number of children in each range

number of children

range of marks in a test

see also chart

hollow

A shape that has nothing inside is hollow.

a hollow pentagonal prism

see also solid

horizontal

A horizontal line is parallel to the horizon or ground. A table has a horizontal top.

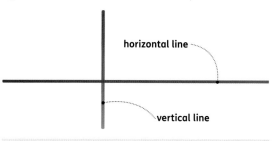

horizontal line

vertical line

see also vertical

hour

An hour is a measurement of time. There are 24 hours in one day. An hour is divided up into minutes and seconds.

1 hour has passed

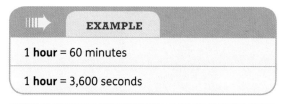

EXAMPLE

1 **hour** = 60 minutes

1 **hour** = 3,600 seconds

see also minute, month

a b c d e f g h i j k l m n o p q r s t u v w x y z

hundredth

❶ One-hundredth ($\frac{1}{100}$) is a fraction showing a whole divided into 100 equal parts.

❷ Hundredth (100th) is an ordinal number showing the 100th position.

> **EXAMPLE**
>
> A cent is a **hundredth** of a dollar.

see also fraction, ordinal number

Ii

I

The Romans used the letter I to stand for the number 1.

> **EXAMPLE**
>
> | I | V | X | L | C | D | M |
> |---|---|---|---|---|---|---|
> | I | = | 1 | | | | |
> | II | = | 2 | | | | |
> | III | = | 3 | | | | |
> | IV | = | 4 | | | | |

see also Roman numerals

icosahedron (*plural* icosahedra)

An icosahedron is a 3D shape that has 20 flat faces. A regular icosahedron has 20 faces that are identical equilateral triangles.

a regular icosahedron

see also triangle, polyhedron, three-dimensional shape

identical

When two or more shapes are identical they have the same shape, size and colour.

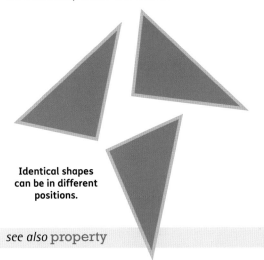

Identical shapes can be in different positions.

see also property

imperial units

Imperial units are measurements such as feet and inches, pints and gallons, pounds and ounces. They are still used in countries such as the US and the UK. Many countries now use a more modern system of measurements called metric units.

EXAMPLE

Capacity

8 pints	=	1 gallon

Length

12 inches	=	1 foot
3 feet	=	1 yard
1,760 yards	=	1 mile

Mass

16 ounces	=	1 pound
14 pounds	=	1 stone
112 pounds	=	1 hundredweight
20 hundredweight	=	1 ton

see also foot, gallon, inch, metric units, ounce, pint, pound

improper fraction *see* fraction

inch

An inch is an imperial unit used to measure length. Twelve inches measure the same as one foot. An inch measures about $2\frac{1}{2}$ cm.

EXAMPLE

12 **inches** = 1 foot

1 **inch** = 2.54 cm

see also foot

increase

When you increase something you make it more or larger.

EXAMPLE

Increase 65 by 15 to get 80.

65 + 15 = 80

see also addition

index (*plural* indices)

Index notation, sometimes called the 'power', is used to tell you the number of times a number is multiplied by itself. These indices are the small digits written to the top right of a number.

EXAMPLE

32 can be written as 2^5

$2 \times 2 \times 2 \times 2 \times 2 = 32$

2 to the power of 5 is 32.

The **index** is 5.

see also cube, square, power, exponent

a b c d e f g h i j k l m n o p q r s t u v w x y z

indirect proportion

If a change in one quantity causes an opposite change in another quantity, we say that the quantities are in indirect proportion. This is also called inverse proportion.

see also direct proportion

inequality

An inequality is when two numbers are not worth the same. The symbols used to show inequality are < > and ≠.

EXAMPLE

12 > 9
12 is greater than 9.

56 < 62
56 is less than 62.

4 + 6 ≠ 9
4 plus 6 does not equal 9.

All these are **inequalities**.

see also equal, greater than, less than, symbol, unequal

infinity

Infinity means going on forever. The counting numbers go on forever, they never stop. Counting goes on to infinity. The symbol for infinity is ∞.

EXAMPLE

0   1   2   ...   345   ...   12,780   ...
53,667,867   ...   ∞

Counting numbers go on forever to **infinity**.

input value

The input value is the number that is entered into a formula or flow diagram.

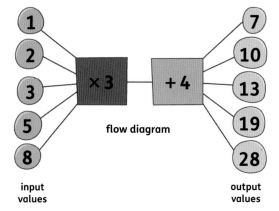

flow diagram

input values   output values

EXAMPLE

The numbers 1, 2, 3, 5 and 8 are the **input values** in the flow diagram.

see also diagram, output value

integer

An integer is any whole number.
An integer can be a positive or a negative number.
Zero is also an integer.

−4   −3   −2   −1   0   1   2   3   4
negative integers   positive integers

0 is also an integer.

see also number

interest

Interest is payment for using money. If you borrow money you pay interest. If you lend money you receive interest. Interest is usually written as a percentage called the interest rate.

EXAMPLE

Borrow £100.
5% **interest** rate.
Repay £105.
The **interest** paid is £5.

Lend £100.
12% **interest** rate.
Receive £112.
The **interest** received is £12.

see also per cent

interior angle *see* angle

intersect

Lines intersect when they cross each other. Intersecting lines can be straight or curved.

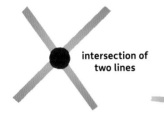
intersection of
two lines

These arcs are
intersecting in
two places.

➤ **intersection**
The point where intersecting lines cross is called the intersection.

interval

An interval is the amount of time or space between two things.

EXAMPLE

6   9   12   15

The **interval** between these numbers is 3.

inverse

❶ If you turn something upside down you have its inverse.
❷ Inverse means reversing something.
Addition and subtraction are inverse operations. Multiplication and division are also inverse operations. The inverse undoes the previous calculation.

EXAMPLE

The **inverse** of $\frac{3}{4}$ is $\frac{4}{3}$.

The **inverse** of + 7 is − 7.
17 + 7 − 7 = 17

The **inverse** of × 4 is ÷ 4.
17 × 4 ÷ 4 = 17

inverse proportion *see* direct proportion

irrational number *see* number

irregular polygon *see* polygon

isosceles triangle *see* triangle

IV

In Roman numerals the number 4 is written as IV (not IIII). When I is placed before another letter you subtract one from the value of the letter.

EXAMPLE			
IV	=	4	(1 before 5)
XIV	=	14	(10 and 1 before 5)
LIV	=	54	(50 and 1 before 5)
CIV	=	104	(100 and 1 before 5)

see also Roman numerals

IX

Usually, the number 9 is written as the Roman numeral IX (not VIIII). When I is placed before another letter you subtract one from the value of the letter.

EXAMPLE			
IX	=	9	(1 before 10)
XIX	=	19	(10 and 1 before 10)
LIX	=	59	(50 and 1 before 10)
CIX	=	109	(100 and 1 before 10)

see also Roman numerals

Jj

join

When you join two points you draw a straight line between them.

A and B have been joined.

junction

A junction is where two or more lines meet.

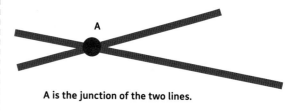

A is the junction of the two lines.

see also intersect, vertex

justify

When trying to prove or disprove an argument or idea, you justify your reasoning by providing good evidence to support it.

EXAMPLE
'I think that all square numbers can be made by adding consecutive odd numbers.'
Can you provide evidence to **justify** the above statement?

kilo-

Kilo- is used as a prefix to show the number 1,000.

 EXAMPLE

1,000 grams is equal to 1 **kilo**gram.

kilogram (*also* kg)

A kilogram is a metric unit of mass used for weighing. There are 1,000 grams in 1 kilogram.

1 kg weighs about the same as 10 large eating apples.

see also gram, metric units, tonne

kilometre (*also* km)

A kilometre is a metric unit of length used to measure long distances. There are 1,000 m in 1 km.

EXAMPLE

It takes about 10 minutes to walk 1 **km**.

see also metre, metric units, speed

kite

A kite is a four-sided polygon. It has two pairs of adjacent sides that are the same length.
A regular polygon also has a pair of angles that are the same.

see also adjacent, polygon, quadrilateral, two-dimensional shape

a
b
c
d
e
f
g
h
i
j
k
l
m
n
o
p
q
r
s
t
u
v
w
x
y
z

L

The Romans used the letter L to stand for the number 50.

EXAMPLE

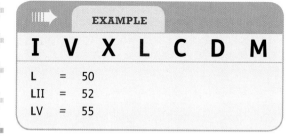

I	V	X	L	C	D	M

L = 50
LII = 52
LV = 55

see also Roman numerals

label

When you give something a label you give it a name. A label tells you what something is. A title is a sort of label.

favourite animals

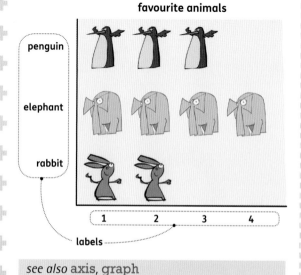

penguin

elephant

rabbit

| 1 | 2 | 3 | 4 |

labels

see also axis, graph

LCD
see lowest common denominator

LCM see lowest common multiple

leap year

A leap year has 29 days in February. This happens every fourth year. There are 366 days in a leap year. Leap years happen because it takes approximately $365\frac{1}{4}$ days for the earth to orbit the Sun, not 365 days.

EXAMPLE

1972 2000 2004 2116
These dates are **leap years**.

Usually if you can divide the year exactly by 4 it is a **leap year**.

see also calendar, date, month, year

length

❶ Length is the measurement along a line or curve. When you measure the length and width of something, the length is usually the longer distance.

The length of both lines is the same.

see also breadth, dimension, height, width

❷ You can measure a length of time in seconds, minutes, hours, days, weeks, months or years.

EXAMPLE

5 seconds is a short **length** of time.

150 years is a long **length** of time.

see also time

less than

Less than means not so many as or fewer than. It also means smaller than. The symbol for less than is **<**. The smaller number always comes before the symbol.

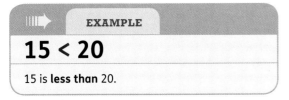

EXAMPLE

15 < 20

15 is **less than** 20.

see also greater than, inequality, symbol

like fractions *see* fraction

line

A line is usually used to mean a straight line. However, a line can also be curved. If you are asked to draw a line between two points always draw a straight line.

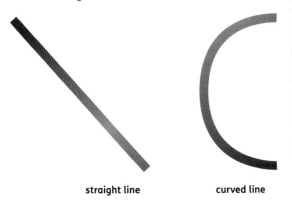

straight line   **curved line**

see also curve, intersect, parallel, straight line

line graph *see* graph

line of symmetry

A line of symmetry divides a shape in half. One half is the reflection of the other half. The line of symmetry is the same as a mirror line. Some shapes have no lines of symmetry while others have one or more.

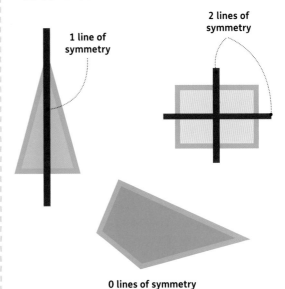

1 line of symmetry

2 lines of symmetry

0 lines of symmetry

see also mirror line, reflect, symmetry

line symmetry *see* symmetry

list

When you make a list you write things underneath each other. Sometimes you put a list in an order.

Shopping List

apples
cheese
bread
socks

a shopping list

a b c d e f g h i j k l m n o p q r s t u v w x y z

litre (*also* l)

A litre is a metric unit used to measure capacity or volume. It is usually used for measuring liquids. The short way of writing litre is l.

EXAMPLE
1 **litre** = 1,000 millilitres
1 l = 1,000 ml
1 **litre** = 100 centilitres
1 l = 100 cl
1 **litre** = 10 decilitres
1 l = 10 dl

1 litre ·········· [measuring cup showing 1,000 ml, 800, 600, 400, 200, 0]

long division

Long division is the type of division where you write out all the calculations for each line. This is useful when dividing larger numbers.

EXAMPLE

$136 \div 4 = 34$

| $\begin{array}{r} 3\,4 \\ 4\,)\overline{1\,3\,6} \\ -1\,2 \\ \hline 1\,6 \\ -1\,6 \\ \hline 0\,0 \end{array}$ | 4 does not go into 1, so look at the next digit and work with 13.
 $4 \times 3 = 12$
 Write 3 at the top and subtract 12 from 13 to get the remainder 1.
 Bring down the next number 6 to make 16.
 $4 \times 4 = 16$
 Write 4 at the top and 16 at the bottom to complete the subtraction. |

see also division

long multiplication

Long multiplication is the type of multiplication where you write out all the calculations for each line. This is useful for multiplying larger numbers.

EXAMPLE

$87 \times 25 = 2,175$

| $\begin{array}{r} 8\,7 \\ \times 2\,5 \\ \hline 4\,3\,5 \\ +1,7\,4\,0 \\ \hline 2,1\,7\,5 \end{array}$ | Multiply by 5
 $87 \times 5 = 435$
 Multiply by 20 (put 0 in the ones column, then multiply by 2)
 $87 \times 20 = 1,740$
 Add the two rows
 $435 + 1,740 = 2,175$ |

see also multiplication

loop

A loop is a line or shape that bends round. A loop often returns to its starting point.

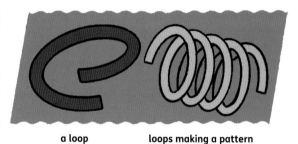

a loop   loops making a pattern

loss

You make a loss when you sell something for less than you paid for it. The loss is the difference between the buying and selling prices.

EXAMPLE
Price paid to buy an item €10.
Price received selling the item €8.
Loss €2.

lowest common denominator
(*also* LCD)

The lowest common denominator (LCD) is the lowest common multiple of the denominators in a set of two or more fractions.

> **EXAMPLE**
>
> Which is the largest fraction out of $\frac{2}{3}$, $\frac{3}{5}$ and $\frac{7}{10}$?
>
> When we compare fractions it is useful to change them so they all have the same denominators. To do this we find the **lowest common denominator**.
>
> 30 is the LCD of 3, 5 and 10.
>
> | $\frac{2}{3} = \frac{20}{30}$ | $\frac{3}{5} = \frac{18}{30}$ | $\frac{7}{10} = \frac{21}{30}$ |
> |---|---|---|
>
> $\frac{7}{10}$ is the largest fraction.

see also common denominator, denominator, lowest common multiple

lowest common multiple
(*also* LCM)

The lowest common multiple (LCM) of two numbers is the smallest number that is a multiple of both numbers.

> **EXAMPLE**
>
> Multiples of 6 are
> 6   12   18   24   30   ...
>
> Multiples of 8 are
> 8   16   24   32   40   ...
>
> Common multiples of 6 and 8 are
> 24   48   72   ...
>
> The **lowest common multiple** is 24.

see also highest common factor, multiple

lowest terms

If a fraction is in its lowest terms it is in its simplest form, so that the only common factor of both the numerator and the denominator is 1.

> **EXAMPLE**
>
> $\frac{12}{15}$ in its **lowest terms** is $\frac{4}{5}$.
>
> Both the numerator and denominator have been divided by 3 and cannot be divided any further by one common factor or number. So the fraction is in its **lowest terms**.

see also cancel, fraction, simplify, simplest form

a b c d e f g h i j k l m n o p q r s t u v w x y z

M

The Romans used the letter M to stand for the number 1,000.

⇒	EXAMPLE	

I	V	X	L	C	D	M

M	=	1,000
MD	=	1,500
MCCXV	=	1,215
MM	=	2,000

see also **Roman numerals**

magic square

In a magic square all the numbers in each row, column and diagonal have the same total.

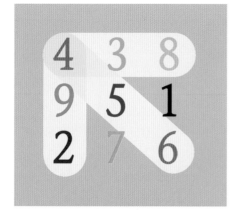

In this magic square each row, column and diagonal totals 15.

see also **column, diagonal, row**

mapping

A mapping is when you join two sets. You pair each member of one set with a member of the second set using a rule.

These are mappings:

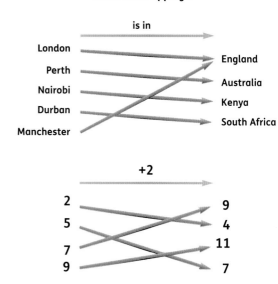

see also **rule, set**

mass

Mass is the amount of matter or material in an object. An elephant has more mass than a cat. Mass and weight are closely linked but are not the same. Weight is the measurement of the force of gravity on an object and is related to its mass. Metric units of mass are grams, kilograms and tonnes.

An astronaut's mass is the same on Earth as on the Moon.

An astronaut will weigh less on the Moon than on Earth but their mass will stay the same.

see also metric units, weight

maximum

The maximum is the largest number in a set. The maximum is the largest possible size, amount or value.

EXAMPLE
19°C   23°C   21°C   18°C
The **maximum** temperature was 23°C.
This was the highest temperature that was recorded.

OPPOSITE The opposite of maximum is minimum.

see also minimum

mean *see* average

measure

❶ A measure is the size of something using a measuring unit. The measuring units are usually metric or imperial.

❷ To measure something is to find out its size using a measuring unit. When you have measured something you record the measurement.

James measured Lisa's height. The measurement was 97 cm.

see also imperial units, metric units

➤ measurement

A measurement is the size of something using a measuring unit. Measurements can be in, for example, grams, metres, seconds or degrees.

median

❶ *see* average

❷ Median is the name given to a line drawn from a corner of a triangle to the middle of the opposite side.

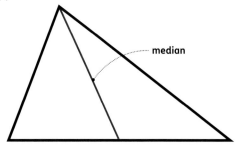

median

see also triangle

mega-

Mega- is used as a prefix to show the number 1 million (1,000,000).

> **EXAMPLE**
>
> A **mega**byte (MB) is one million bytes of digital information.

see also giga-

mental calculation

A mental calculation is one that can be carried out in your head using recall of facts or a strategy to reach the answer.

> **EXAMPLE**
>
> Can you answer this **mental calculation**?
>
> 98 + 102 = ?
>
> Answer: 200

metre (*also* m)

A metre is a metric unit used to measure length or distance. The short way of writing metre is m.

> **EXAMPLE**
>
> | |
> |---|
> | 1 **metre** = 1,000 millimetres |
> | 1 **m** = 1,000 mm |
> | 1 **metre** = 100 centimetres |
> | 1 **m** = 100 cm |
> | 1 **metre** = 10 decimetres |
> | 1 **m** = 10 dm |
> | 1,000 **metres** = 1 kilometre |
> | 1,000 **m** = 1 km |

see also centimetre, decimetre, kilometre, metric units, millimetre

metric ton (*also* tonne)

A metric ton is 1,000 kilograms. A metric ton is also called a tonne.

> **EXAMPLE**
>
> 1,000 kilograms = 1 **tonne**
>
> A tonne is the same as a **metric ton**.

see also kilogram, metric units, tonne

metric units

Metric units are part of the metric system of measurement. The units are based on tens, hundreds and thousands. Metric units started to be used at the time of the French Revolution.

> **EXAMPLE**
>
> | Capacity: | Length: | Mass: |
> |---|---|---|
> | millilitre | millimetre | gram |
> | centilitre | centimetre | kilogram |
> | decilitre | decimetre | tonne |
> | litre | metre | |
> | | kilometre | |

see also centimetre, gram, kilogram, kilometre, litre, metre, millilitre, millimetre, imperial units

mid-

Mid is short for middle. Words such as midday, midsummer and midpoint all have something to do with middle.

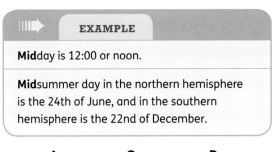

> **EXAMPLE**
>
> **Mid**day is 12:00 or noon.
>
> **Mid**summer day in the northern hemisphere is the 24th of June, and in the southern hemisphere is the 22nd of December.

A   C   B

C is the midpoint between A and B.

see also midday, midnight

midday

Midday is the middle of the day. It is another name for noon. Midday happens 12 hours after midnight. Midday is the time when a.m. times become p.m. times.

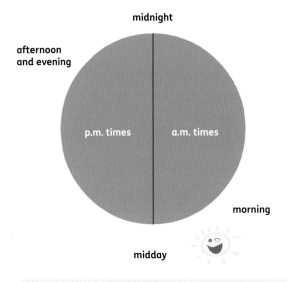

see also a.m., midnight, p.m.

midnight

Midnight is the middle of the night. Midnight happens 12 hours after midday. Midnight is the time when p.m. times become a.m. times. Using a 24 hour clock midnight is 24:00 or 00:00; both of these are correct.

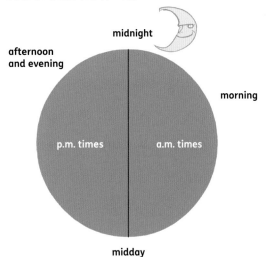

see also a.m., midday, p.m.

mile

A mile is an imperial unit used to measure long distances. The distance got its name from the Latin *mille passus* which meant a thousand paces. It takes about 15 minutes to walk 1 mile. 1 mile is approximately 1,600 m.

> **EXAMPLE**
>
> 1 **mile** = 1,760 yards
>
> 1 **mile** = 1,609.344 metres
>
> 5 **miles** ≈ 8 kilometres

see also imperial units, yard

millennium

A millennium is one thousand years.

> **EXAMPLE**
>
> The year 2,000 was the beginning of the third **millennium** AD.
>
> The year 3,000 will be the beginning of the fourth **millennium** AD.

see also century

milli-

Milli- is used as a prefix to show the number $\frac{1}{1,000}$.

> **EXAMPLE**
>
> A **millimetre** is $\frac{1}{1,000}$ of a metre.

see also centi-

millilitre (*also* ml)

A millilitre is a metric unit used to measure a small capacity or volume. There are 1,000 millilitres in 1 litre. A teaspoon holds about 5 ml.

> **EXAMPLE**
>
> 1,000 **millilitres** = 1 litre
>
> 100 **millilitres** = 1 decilitre
>
> 10 **millilitres** = 1 centilitre

5 millilitres

see also centilitre, decilitre, litre, metric units

millimetre (*also* mm)

A millimetre is a metric unit used to measure a small length or distance. There are 1,000 mm in 1 m. The short way of writing millimetre is mm.

> **EXAMPLE**
>
> 1,000 **millimetres** = 1 metre
>
> 1,000 **mm** = 1 m
>
> 100 **millimetres** = 1 decimetre
>
> 100 **mm** = 1 dm
>
> 10 **millimetres** = 1 centimetre
>
> 10 **mm** = 1 cm

see also centimetre, metre, metric units

million

A million is a large number. It is one thousand thousands. You write it as one followed by six zeros. A million is a seven digit number.

> **EXAMPLE**
>
> 1 **million** = 1,000,000

see also billion, digit, place value

minimum

The minimum is the smallest number in a set. The minimum is the smallest possible size, amount or value.

−1°C   −3°C   0°C   −2°C

The minimum temperature was −1°C.

This was the lowest temperature that was recorded.

OPPOSITE The opposite of minimum is maximum.

see also maximum

minuend

The minuend is the number at the start of a subtraction calculation, which then has an amount subtracted from it.

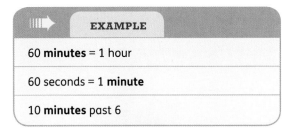

EXAMPLE
60 − 40 = 20
60 is the **minuend**.
40 is the subtrahend.
20 is the difference.

see also subtraction, subtrahend

minus

Minus is the name for the subtraction symbol **−**.

EXAMPLE
3 − 2 = 1
Three **minus** two equals one.

3 − 2 = 1
3 minus 2
equals 1.

see also plus, symbol

minute

A minute is a measurement of time. There are 60 minutes in 1 hour. A minute can be divided up into 60 seconds. Some analogue clocks show hours, minutes and seconds but some clocks only show hours and minutes.

EXAMPLE
60 **minutes** = 1 hour
60 seconds = 1 **minute**
10 **minutes** past 6

minute hand

see also analogue, hour, second

mirror line

A mirror line is a line of symmetry. The shape on one side of the mirror line is the reflection of the shape on the other side. If you fold along the mirror line one half of the shape will fold exactly on top of the other half.

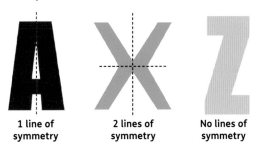

1 line of symmetry	2 lines of symmetry	No lines of symmetry

The dotted lines are mirror lines or lines of symmetry.

see also line symmetry, reflection, symmetry

a b c d e f g h i j k l m n o p q r s t u v w x y z

mirror symmetry *see* symmetry

mixed number *see* number

mode *see* average

month

There are twelve months in one year.
A calendar month has 28, 29, 30 or 31 days.

> **EXAMPLE**
>
> The 12 **months** are:
>
> | | |
> |---|---|
> | January
31 days | July
31 days |
> | February
28/29 days | August
31 days |
> | March
31 days | September
30 days |
> | April
30 days | October
31 days |
> | May
31 days | November
30 days |
> | June
30 days | December
31 days |
>
> One **month** from 25th May is 25th June.

see also calendar, year

more than *see* greater than

morning

The time between midnight and midday is called the morning. Morning times are a.m. times.

9:00 a.m.

nine o'clock in the morning

see also afternoon, a.m., evening

multiple

A multiple is a number that contains another number (a factor) an exact amount of times with no remainder. 12 is a multiple of 3 as it is made up of four 3s (3 × 4 = 12). Multiples are like multiplication tables.

> **EXAMPLE**
>
> **Multiples** of 3 are:
> 3 6 9 12 15 ...
>
> **Multiples** of 5 are:
> 5 10 15 20 25 ...
>
> **Multiples** of 12 are:
> 12 24 36 48 60 ...
>
> **Multiples** do not stop at the tenth, they go on and on.

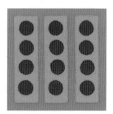

multiples of 3

see also lowest common multiple, multiply

multiplicand

The multiplicand is a number that is multiplied by a multiplier. It is the first number in a written multiplication sentence.

EXAMPLE

3 × 5 = 15

3 is the **multiplicand**.

5 is the multiplier.

15 is the product.

The **multiplicand** and the multiplier are also called the factors of a number.

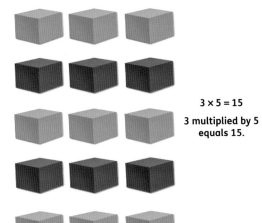

3 × 5 = 15

3 multiplied by 5 equals 15.

see also factor, multiplier, product

multiplication

Multiplication is adding lots of the same number together. The symbol for multiplication is ×.

EXAMPLE

6 × 3 = 18

This is the **multiplication** of 6 by 3.

This is the same as three lots of sixes:
6 + 6 + 6 = 18

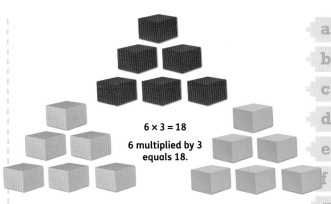

6 × 3 = 18

6 multiplied by 3
equals 18.

see also multiple, multiply

multiplier

A multiplier is a number that multiplies another number, called the multiplicand.

EXAMPLE

4 × 5 = 20

4 is the multiplicand.

5 is the **multiplier**.

20 is the product.

The multiplicand and the **multiplier** are also called the factors of a number.

4 × 5 = 20

4 multiplied by 5 equals 20.

see also factor, multiplicand, product

a b c d e f g h i j k l m n o p q r s t u v w x y z

multiply

When you multiply something you increase it a number of times. Multiplying refers to the same operation as multiplication.

EXAMPLE

Multiply 4 by 4 means 4×4.

$4 \times 4 = 16$

4 **multiplied** by 4 equals 16.

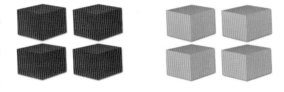

$4 \times 4 = 16$
4 multiplied by 4 equals 16.

see also multiple, multiplication

Nn

natural number *see* number

near

When something is near it is very close to something. Other words that can mean the same as near are close to, nearly touching, next to, almost.

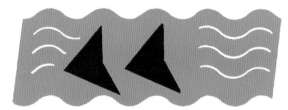

The two shapes are near to each other.

➤ **nearly**

Nearly means almost.

▌▌▌➡ **EXAMPLE**

48 is **near** 50.

48 is **nearly** 50.

see also approximate

negative number *see* number

net

A net is a flat shape that you can fold up to make a solid shape. The net shows what a shape looks like once it has been opened out and flattened.

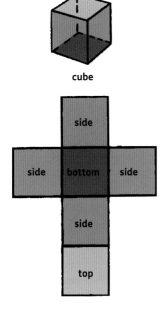

cube

the net of a cube

A cube has several different nets.

see also flat shape, solid

night

Night is the dark part of the day. It is the time between sunset and sunrise.

Midnight is in the middle of the night.

see also afternoon, day, evening, morning

nonagon

A nonagon is any 2D shape that has nine straight sides. A regular nonagon has all its sides and angles the same size.

regular nonagon

irregular nonagon

see also plane shape, polygon, two-dimensional shape

none

None means not one, nothing at all.

The left plate has four oranges but the right has none.

see also zero

non-unit fraction *see* fraction

nought (*also* zero)

Nought is another word for zero, nothing or none. It is written as the number 0.

EXAMPLE

3,050   0.005

Noughts are important in place value.

negative numbers   positive numbers

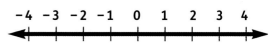
−4 −3 −2 −1   0   1   2   3   4

Nought separates negative and positive numbers.

see also place value, zero

a b c d e f g h i j k l m **n** o p q r s t u v w x y z

number

We use numbers to count quantity or to measure.
Numbers have a position on a number line.
There are many different kinds of number.

see also digit, integer, number line

cardinal number

A cardinal number is any whole number that
we use for counting. They are numbers that
show how many there are in a set, but not the
order they are in.

2   6   7   19
These are all **cardinal numbers** as they can be
used to count how many there are in a set.

composite number

A composite number is any number with three
or more factors. This means it cannot be 0, 1
or a prime number.

4   6   8   9   10   12
These are all **composite numbers**.

even number

An even number is any whole number that
can be divided by 2 exactly, without leaving
a remainder.

2   18   56   176   3086
These are all **even numbers**.

see also divisible

irrational number

Irrational numbers are those numbers that
cannot be written as rational numbers. They
are never-ending numbers, only written with
non-repeating decimals.

Pi (π) is an example of an **irrational number**. »

natural number

A natural number is any whole number that
we use for counting. They are only positive
whole numbers and can include zero.

1   2   3   4   5   6
These are all **natural numbers**.

negative number

Negative numbers are less than zero.
On a number line they are to the left of zero.
Negative numbers have the minus sign in
front of them.

You can write the **negative number** two as −2.

see also minus, number line, sign

odd number

An odd number is any whole number that
cannot be divided by 2 exactly and will leave
a remainder. An odd number is a whole
number that is not even.

3   17   59   171   3089
These are all **odd numbers**.

see also divisible

ordinal number

Ordinal numbers are numbers such as first,
second, third, fourth. An ordinal number tells
you the position of something.

Ordinal numbers are sometimes written
like this:
1st   2nd   3rd   4th   5th   »

perfect number

A perfect number is any number that is the sum of all its factors, not including the actual number.

6 is a **perfect number**.

1 + 2 + 3 = 6
What is the next **perfect number** after 6?

Answer: 28 (1 + 2 + 4 + 7 + 14)

see also factor

positive number

Positive numbers are more than zero. On a number line they are to the right of zero. Positive numbers have the plus sign in front of them.

You can write the **positive number** two as +2.

see also number line, sign

prime number

A prime number has only two factors which are 1 and itself. One is not a prime number because it has only one factor not two.

2   3   5   7   11   13   17   19
These are all the **prime numbers** between 1 and 20.

see also Eratosthenes sieve, factor

rational number

Rational numbers are those numbers that can be written as a fraction in the form of $\frac{a}{b}$ where a and b are both integers.

−6   8   0.7   0.05   7.3333
These are all **rational numbers** because they can be written as:

$$\frac{-6}{1} \qquad \frac{8}{1} \qquad \frac{7}{10} \qquad \frac{1}{20} \qquad \frac{22}{3}$$

see also fraction, integer   »

square number

A square number is the product of two identical whole numbers. When a number is squared it is multiplied by itself.

1   9   16   25
These are all **square numbers**.

see also squared, square root

triangle numbers
see triangular numbers

whole number

Whole numbers are the numbers you use to count with. Whole numbers are the positive integers including zero. A fraction is not a whole number.

0   1   2   3   4   5
Whole numbers go on to infinity.

see also infinity, integer

number bonds

Number bonds are pairs of numbers that add together to make a total.

 EXAMPLE

The **number bonds** for 7 are

0 + 7   1 + 6   2 + 5   3 + 4.

number line

A number line is a line with a scale to show the order and position of numbers. It is a continuous line with values between each number along the line.

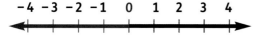

negative numbers   positive numbers

−4 −3 −2 −1   0   1   2   3   4

 EXAMPLE

This **number line** goes from 0 to 10.

number sentence

A number sentence is a mathematical sentence. It uses numbers, words and symbols.

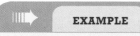 **EXAMPLE**

6 subtract 4 leaves 2.

[ ] + 5 = 14   8 > 3

These are all **number sentences**.

see also equation

number track

A number track is a continuous track with numbers written in the spaces. A value is given to each space on the track, but not between the spaces.

1	2	3	4	5	6

see also number line

numeral

A numeral is any symbol or word for a number.

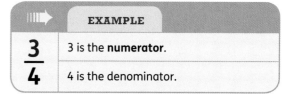

3 three III

These are all numerals.

see also digit, number, Roman numerals

numerator

The top number of a fraction is called the numerator. The numerator tells you how many equal parts there are.

EXAMPLE

$\dfrac{3}{4}$ 3 is the **numerator**.

4 is the denominator.

see also denominator, fraction

Oo

oblique
Oblique lines are sloping or slanting. They are not horizontal or vertical.

oblique lines

see also horizontal, vertical

oblong
An oblong is a shape that is longer than it is wide. Rectangles can be oblongs.

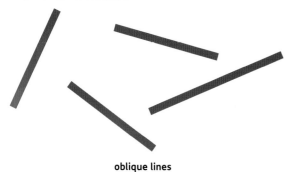

an oblong rectangle   an oblong with rounded corners

see also polygon, quadrilateral, rectangle

obtuse angle *see* angle

obtuse-angled triangle
see triangle

octagon
An octagon is any polygon that has eight straight sides. In a regular octagon all the sides and angles are equal.

regular octagon   irregular octagon

see also polygon, two-dimensional shape

➤ octagonal
Octagonal shapes have eight sides.

octahedron
(*plural* octahedra)
An octahedron is any solid shape that has eight flat faces. A regular octahedron has eight equilateral triangle faces.

regular octahedron

see also polyhedron, solid

odd number *see* number

operation
An operation is when you change a number by adding, subtracting, multiplying or dividing. The operation symbols are **+ − ×** and **÷**.

EXAMPLE

| 12 + 5 | 12 − 8 | 12 × 4 | 12 ÷ 6 |

All these are **operations** on the number 12.

see also addition, divide, multiply, subtraction

order

Order is the way things are arranged. You often put things in order of size or quantity. The alphabet is an order for letters. Numbers are often arranged in order of size, either going up in ascending order, or going down in descending order.

> **EXAMPLE**
>
> 2   6   13   17   22
> ascending **order**
>
> 30 cm   21 cm   19 cm   10 cm   8 cm
> descending **order**

see also ascending, descending

ordered pair

An ordered pair is a pair of numbers taken together, where the order of the two numbers is very important. Coordinates are an example of an ordered pair. They are often written in brackets.

> **EXAMPLE**
>
> In an **ordered pair** (2,3) is different to (3,2).
>
> These **ordered pairs** are at different positions on a graph.
>
> (2,3) is 2 along (on the horizontal axis) and 3 up (on the vertical axis).
>
> (3,2) is 3 along (on the horizontal axis) and 2 up (on the vertical axis).

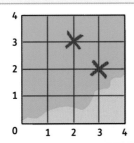

see also coordinate

order of operations

The order of operations in a calculation is a set of rules used to make sure that consistent answers are given by carrying out the different parts of the calculation in a certain order.

> **EXAMPLE**
>
> $(3 + 5) \times 3 - 1 = 23$
> $8 \times 3 - 1 = 23$
> $24 - 1 = 23$
>
> Anything in brackets is done first, then indices, followed by division and multiplication, and finally addition and subtraction.
>
> BIDMAS is used to remember this:
> Brackets, Indices, Division, Multiplication, Addition, Subtraction

order of rotational symmetry

The order of rotational symmetry of a shape is the number of times it will fit into its outline when being rotated.

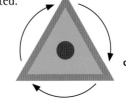

An equilateral triangle has an order of rotational symmetry of 3.

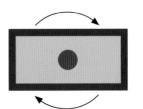

A rectangle has an order of rotational symmetry of 2.

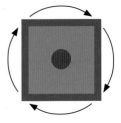

A square has an order of rotational symmetry of 4.

see also symmetry

ordinal number *see* number

origin

The origin is where something starts. On a graph the origin is where the two axes cross, usually with the coordinates (0,0).

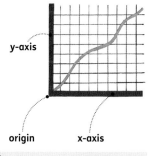

y-axis

origin   x-axis

see also axis, coordinate

ounce (also oz)

An ounce is an imperial unit of weight or mass. The short way of writing ounce is oz. 1 oz is about 28 g.

 EXAMPLE

| 16 **ounces** = 1 pound | 1 **ounce** = 28.3 grams |
| 16 **oz** = 1 lb | 1 **oz** = 28.3 g |

see also imperial units, pound

output value

The output value is the number that is determined by a formula or flow diagram.

 EXAMPLE

13 is the **output value** that corresponds to the input number 3 in the flow diagram.

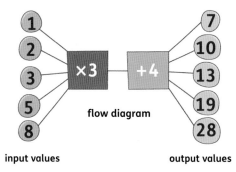

flow diagram

input values   output values

see also diagram, input value

oval

An oval is a 2D shape like a flattened circle. There are two types of oval. One oval is egg-shaped with one end more pointed than the other. The other oval which has the same curve at both ends is called an ellipse. Ovals can be symmetrical or asymmetrical.

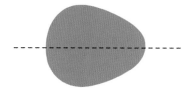

This oval is egg-shaped with 1 line of symmetry.

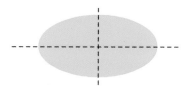

This oval is an ellipse with 2 lines of symmetry.

see also ellipse, symmetry, asymmetrical

ovoid

An ovoid is a 3D shape that looks like an egg. It is like a sphere with one end that is more pointed than the rest of the shape.

an ovoid

see also three-dimensional shape

a
b
c
d
e
f
g
h
i
j
k
l
m
n
o
p
q
r
s
t
u
v
w
x
y
z

Pp

pace

A pace is an informal measurement. It is the length of one step when you walk normally.

a pace

pair

A pair is two of anything.

a pair of shoes

see also factor pair, ordered pair

palindrome

A palindrome is any word or number that is the same when it is read forwards and backwards.

➤ palindromic

Palindromic means in the form of a palindrome.

 EXAMPLE

2002 was a **palindromic** year.
The next **palindromic** year is 2112.

palm

A palm is an old measuring unit. It is the width of a hand. It does not include the thumb.

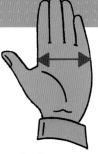

A palm measures 4 finger widths.

parallel

Parallel lines are the same distance apart no matter how long they are. Parallel lines can never cross each other.

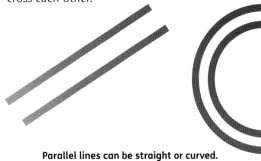

Parallel lines can be straight or curved.

see also parallelogram

parallelogram

A parallelogram is a four-sided shape that has its opposite sides parallel to each other.

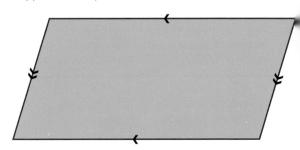

The arrowheads show which sides are parallel to each other.

see also rectangle, rhombus

partition

When a number is partitioned it is separated into different parts. Partitioning is the act of separating a set into subsets.

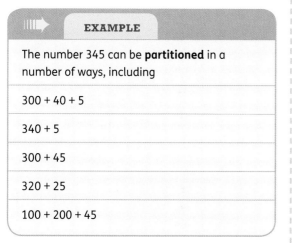

EXAMPLE

The number 345 can be **partitioned** in a number of ways, including
300 + 40 + 5
340 + 5
300 + 45
320 + 25
100 + 200 + 45

pattern

A pattern is an arrangement of numbers, lines or shapes that follows a rule.

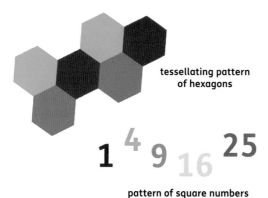

tessellating pattern
of hexagons

1 4 9 16 25

pattern of square numbers

repeating pattern

see also number, tessellate

penny (*also* p)

A penny is a coin and unit of money in the UK. There are 100 pence (100p) in one pound (£1). The short way of writing penny is p.

pentagon

A pentagon is any 2D shape with five straight sides. A regular pentagon has all its sides and angles the same.

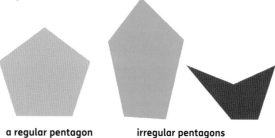

a regular pentagon   irregular pentagons

see also polygon, two-dimensional shape

➤ **pentagonal**

Something that looks like a pentagon is pentagonal.

pentomino

A pentomino is a shape made from arranging five identical squares together. The squares are joined at their sides.

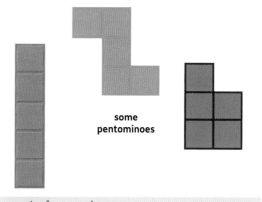

some
pentominoes

see also hexomino

a b c d e f g h i j k l m n o p q r s t u v w x y z

per

Per means for each.

> **EXAMPLE**
>
> A speed of 70 kilometres **per** hour means the vehicle is travelling 70 kilometres in each hour. It may be written as 70 km/h.
>
> 150 cm of rain **per** annum = 150 cm of rain in each year
>
> 5 litres **per** person means each person gets 5 litres.

see also per cent, speed

per cent

Per cent means out of a hundred or for every hundred. The symbol for per cent is **%.**

➤ percentage

A percentage is a number which tells you how many are in each hundred. A percentage is another way of writing a fraction that has a denominator of 100.

> **EXAMPLE**
>
> $50\% = \frac{50}{100} = \frac{1}{2}$
>
> $25\% = \frac{25}{100} = \frac{1}{4}$
>
> $10\% = \frac{10}{100} = \frac{1}{10}$
>
> **Percentages** can be written as fractions.

see also fraction, per

perfect number see number

perimeter

The perimeter is the distance all the way around a shape. You can calculate the perimeter of 2D shapes by adding together the length of the lines that make up the shape. For a circle, the perimeter is its circumference.

> **EXAMPLE**
>
> The **perimeter** of a rectangle which has a length of 5 cm and width of 3 cm is 16 cm.
>
> 5 cm + 3 cm + 5 cm + 3 cm = 16 cm

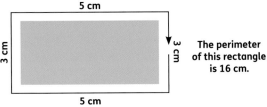

The perimeter of this rectangle is 16 cm.

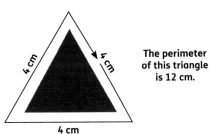

The perimeter of this triangle is 12 cm.

see also circle

perpendicular

Two things are perpendicular when they meet at right angles.

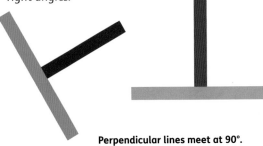

Perpendicular lines meet at 90°.

see also horizontal, vertical

pi (also π)

Pi is slightly bigger than 3. It is the number you get when you divide the circumference of a circle by its diameter. This always comes to the same number. Pi is approximately 3.142 or $\frac{22}{7}$.
The symbol for pi is **π**.

> **EXAMPLE**
>
> $$\frac{\text{circumference}}{\text{diameter}} = π$$
>
> $$\frac{\text{circumference}}{\text{diameter}} \approx 3.142$$
>
> Circumference of a circle $= 2 \times π \times r$
>
> Area of a circle $= π \times r^2$

see also circle

pictogram (also pictograph, picture graph)

In a pictogram pictures are used to stand for quantities. A picture can stand for one thing or a number of things. Pictograms can also be called pictographs or picture graphs.

number of bananas eaten by each chimpanzee

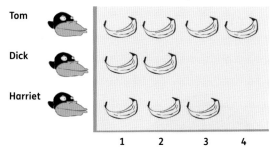

Each picture stands for one banana.

see also graph

pie chart *see* chart

pint

A pint is an imperial unit used to measure capacity. Eight pints make a gallon.
A pint is about half a litre. A litre is about $1\frac{3}{4}$ pints.

> **EXAMPLE**
>
> 8 **pints** = 1 gallon
>
> 1 **pint** = 0.568 litres

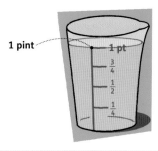

see also gallon, imperial units

place value

Place value is the value a digit has because of its position in a number. The same digit can have different values depending on its position in a number.

> **EXAMPLE**
>
> | 4,346 | 4.346 |
> |-------|-------|
> | value 4,000 | value 4 |
> | 4,346 | 4.346 |
> | value 40 | value $\frac{4}{100}$ |

see also decimal number

plan

A plan is a diagram showing where things are. Plans often have a scale because they cannot be drawn life size. A scale makes sure that each part of the plan or the drawing is the correct size in relation to the other parts.

This is a street plan.

see also scale drawing, proportion

plane

A plane is a flat surface. It can be vertical, horizontal or oblique.

vertical plane   horizontal plane   oblique plane

see also plane shape, symmetry

plane shape (*also* plane figure)

Plane shapes are 2D shapes. They have no thickness. Sometimes plane shapes are called plane figures.

Plane shapes can have straight or curved sides.

see also plane, polygon, two-dimensional shape

plane symmetry *see* symmetry

plot

You plot points on a graph. When you mark a position on a graph you are plotting the coordinates.

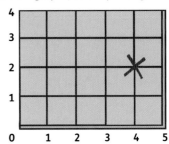

The coordinates (4,2) have been plotted.

see also coordinate

plus

Plus is the name for the addition symbol **+**.

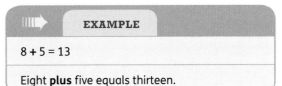

EXAMPLE

8 + 5 = 13

Eight **plus** five equals thirteen.

see also addition, minus, symbol

p.m.

The letters p.m. stand for *post meridiem*, which is Latin for 'after midday'. The letters are used to show times after 12 noon but before 12 midnight.

9:00 p.m.

nine o'clock in the evening

see also afternoon, a.m., evening

point

❶ You plot points on a graph. A point is really like a very small dot but is often marked with a small cross. The point is the middle of the cross.

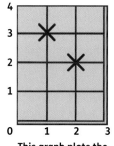

This graph plots the points (1,3) and (2,2).

see also coordinate, plot

❷ *see* compass

point symmetry *see* symmetry

polygon

A polygon is any 2D shape with straight sides. Many polygons have special names. For example, triangles, squares and rectangles are types of polygon. Polygons can be regular or irregular.

⚙ irregular polygon

Irregular polygons do not have all their sides the same length. They have different size angles.

⚙ regular polygon

A regular polygon is any polygon that has all its sides and angles the same. A square is a regular quadrilateral.

see also concave, convex, plane shape, two-dimensional shape

irregular polygons

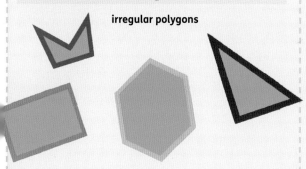

EXAMPLE	
Polygon sides	**Special name**
3 sides	triangle
4 sides	quadrilateral
5 sides	pentagon
6 sides	hexagon
7 sides	heptagon
8 sides	octagon
9 sides	nonagon
10 sides	decagon
12 sides	dodecagon

regular polygons

quadrilateral

pentagon

hexagon

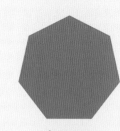

heptagon

octagon

nonagon

a b c d e f g h i j k l m n o p q r s t u v w x y z

polyhedron (*plural* polyhedra)

A polyhedron is any 3D shape made from polygons. Some polyhedra have special names such as cube, pyramid or tetrahedron. Polyhedra have faces, edges and vertices.

○ regular polyhedron

A regular polyhedron is the same as a regular solid or 3D shape. The faces of a regular polyhedron are all identical regular polygons. The faces all meet at the same angle. There are five regular polyhedra called tetrahedron, hexahedron or cube, octahedron, dodecahedron and icosahedron.

> **EXAMPLE**

Type of face	Polyhedron name
4 equilateral triangles	tetrahedron
6 squares	hexahedron or cube
8 equilateral triangles	octahedron
12 pentagons	dodecahedron
20 equilateral triangles	icosahedron

These are the five regular polyhedra.

tetrahedron

hexahedron

octahedron

dodecahedron

icosahedron

see also edge, face, solid, three-dimensional shape, vertex

portion

A portion is a part of a whole. If the portions are equal then they are all the same fraction of a whole.

> **EXAMPLE**

A bar of chocolate has 12 equal **portions**. Each **portion** is $\frac{1}{12}$ of the whole.

position

❶ The position of an object is where it can be found—its place or location.

> **EXAMPLE**

A coordinates grid is used to find the **position** of objects drawn on a grid.

see also coordinate

❷ Position also describes the order in which objects or people are placed.

see also order, number

positive number *see* number

pound

❶ (*also* lb)

A pound is an imperial unit of weight or mass. The short way of writing pound is lb. A pound is divided into 16 ounces. A one-pound weight is about 450 grams. A kilogram is about $2\frac{1}{4}$ pounds.

> **EXAMPLE**

1 **pound** = 16 ounces
1 **lb** = 16 oz
1 **lb** = 453.59 g
1 kg = 2.204 **lb**

see also imperial units, ounce

(*also* £)

A pound is a unit of money in the UK, equal to 100 pennies. The symbol for pound is **£**.

> **EXAMPLE**
>
> 1 **pound** = 100 pennies
>
> £1 = 100p

see also penny

power

You read 3^4 as 3 to the power of 4. It means $3 \times 3 \times 3 \times 3$. The power shows how many equal numbers have been multiplied together. A number to the power of 2 is said to be squared. A number to the power of 3 is said to be cubed.

> **EXAMPLE**
>
> 4^2 is 4 squared or 4 to the **power** of 2.
>
> 4^3 is 4 cubed or 4 to the **power** of 3.

see also cube, index, squared, order of operations, exponent

prime factor

Factors of a number that are also prime numbers are called prime factors.

> **EXAMPLE**
>
> The factors of 24 are 1, 2, 3, 4, 6, 8, 12, 24.
>
> The **prime factors** of 24 are 2 and 3.

see also factor, number

prime number *see* number

prism

A prism is a solid shape with matching ends that are polygons. The cross-section, parallel to the base, of a prism is always the same shape. A prism is also a polyhedron. Cubes and cuboids are special types of prism. The shape of the base gives the prism its name.

> **hexagonal prism**
>
> A prism that has hexagonal ends is called a hexagonal prism.

> **triangular prism**
>
> A triangular prism is a prism that has triangular ends. The end can be any type of triangle.

triangular prism · pentagonal prism · hexagonal prism

see also cross-section, polygon, polyhedron

probability

Probability is the chance of something happening. You often write the probability of something happening as a fraction. Words you might use when talking about probability include: chance, likelihood, odds.

> **EXAMPLE**
>
> Toss a coin.
> The **probability** of getting heads is 1 in 2.
> The **probability** is $\frac{1}{2}$.
>
> Roll a dice.
> The **probability** of getting a six is 1 in 6.
> The **probability** is $\frac{1}{6}$.

see also probability scale, trial

probability scale

A probability scale is a diagram to show the chance of something happening. If something has no chance of happening, it has a probability of 0. If something is certain, it will have a probability of 1. If something has an even chance, the probability is $\frac{1}{2}$ or 0.5.

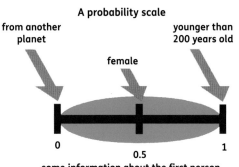

A probability scale

from another planet

younger than 200 years old

female

0   0.5   1

some information about the first person you might see on the street tomorrow

see also probability

probable

If something is probable it will most likely happen. It might not happen but the chances are that it will.

> **EXAMPLE**
>
> It is **probable** that the next person you meet will be right-handed.

see also probability

product

The product is the answer you get by multiplying numbers together.

> **EXAMPLE**
>
> The **product** of 3 and 7 is 21 because 3 × 7 = 21.
>
> The **product** of 2, 4 and 5 is 40 because 2 × 4 × 5 = 40.

see also multiply

profit

Profit is what you make when you sell something for more than you paid for it. The profit is the difference between the buying and selling prices.

> **EXAMPLE**
>
> | Buy for R35. | Buy for £6. |
> | Sell for R50. | Sell for £10. |
> | **Profit** is R15. | **Profit** is £4. |

see also difference, loss, cost price

proper fraction see fraction

property

(*plural* properties)

You talk about the property of something when you describe it. Properties are things such as colour, size and number of sides.

Some properties of this square are: blue, right-angled, equal-sided, four-sided, parallel-sided.

see also attribute

proportion

❶ A scale model is in proportion to the real thing. With a scale of one fifth everything on the model would be one fifth of the real thing. Maps are in proportion to the real measurements on the ground.

see also enlarge, reduce, scale

❷ Numbers can be in proportion. 2 and 6 are in the same proportion as 5 and 15 because in each pair the first number is a third of the second number.

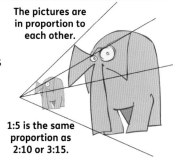

The pictures are in proportion to each other.

1:5 is the same proportion as 2:10 or 3:15.

see also fraction, ratio

pyramid

A pyramid is a solid shape that has a polygon for a base. Each of the sides are triangles meeting at a point. The shape of the base gives the pyramid its name.

○ square-based pyramid

A square-based pyramid has a face that is square. The other four sides are triangles that meet at a point.

see also base, polyhedron

○ triangular pyramid

A triangular pyramid is a pyramid with a triangle at its base. It is another name for a tetrahedron.

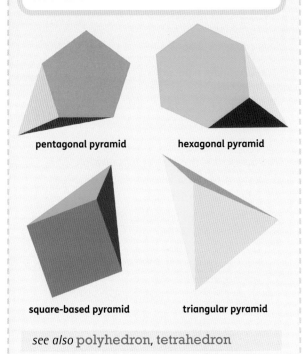

pentagonal pyramid   hexagonal pyramid

square-based pyramid   triangular pyramid

see also polyhedron, tetrahedron

Qq

quadrant

❶ *see* circle

❷ The axes of a graph divide the graph into four quadrants. In the first quadrant both coordinates are positive. In the third quadrant both coordinates are negative.

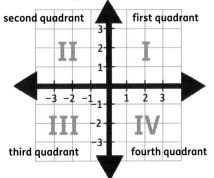

second quadrant   first quadrant

II   I

III   IV

third quadrant   fourth quadrant

see also axis, coordinate

quadrilateral

A quadrilateral is any polygon that has four sides. The four angles of a quadrilateral add up to 360°.

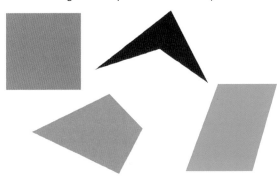

see also polygon, two-dimensional shape

quantity (*plural* quantities)

A quantity is the total number or amount of items. It can usually be measured or counted.

> **EXAMPLE**
>
> Eggs sold in shops are usually in **quantities** of 6, 12 or 20 depending on the size of the boxes.

quart

A quart is an imperial unit used to measure capacity.

> **EXAMPLE**
>
> 1 **quart** = 2 pints
>
> 4 **quarts** = 1 gallon
>
> 1 **quart** = 1.14 litres

see also gallon, imperial units, pint

quarter

A quarter ($\frac{1}{4}$) is one of four equal parts. You can find a quarter of a shape, quantity or number. Two quarters is the same as a half.

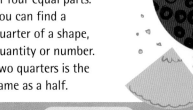

> **EXAMPLE**
>
> $\frac{1}{4}$ of an hour = 15 minutes
>
> $\frac{1}{4}$ of 24 = 6

see also fraction, half

quarter-turn

A quarter-turn is a turn of 90°.

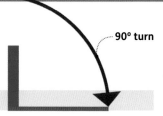

90° turn

see also half-turn

questionnaire

A questionnaire is a printed set of questions. Questionnaires are used to collect information and data. They often have YES/NO answers, boxes to tick or scales to show how much you like things.

> **EXAMPLE**
>
> **Questionnaire** about reading

Do you read every night?	YES/NO
Do you read fiction?	YES/NO
Do you read about sport?	YES/NO
Do you prefer a paperback to a hardback?	YES/NO

quotient

The quotient is the answer to a division. A quotient can be a whole number, fraction, mixed number or decimal.

> **EXAMPLE**

$4\overline{)27}$ 6 r3	6 is the **quotient**.
	3 is the remainder.
$4\overline{)27.00}$ 6.75	6.75 is the **quotient**.
$\frac{27}{4} = 6\frac{3}{4}$	$6\frac{3}{4}$ is the **quotient**.

see also dividend, division, divisor

Rr

radius *see* circle

random

Random means purely by chance. If you choose a number at random you pick any number that you wish. Random numbers do not have an order.

➤ **randomly**

Randomly means at random or purely by chance.

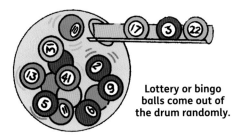

Lottery or bingo balls come out of the drum randomly.

range

The range is the difference between the smallest value and the largest value. You often need to know the range when you are finding averages.

> **EXAMPLE**
>
> 3 3 4 6 9
>
> Here are five numbers from 3 to 9.
>
> The smallest number is 3, the largest is 9.
>
> The **range** is from 3 to 9 which equals 6.

see also average

rate

Rate is a measure of how quickly an amount changes compared to another. It is also a measure of how quickly an event happens.

> **EXAMPLE**
>
> Water flows from a hose at a faster **rate** than from a tap.
>
> If it takes 1 hour to drive 60 km, the **rate** at which the journey was completed is 60 km/h (60 kilometres per hour).

ratio

A ratio is a way of comparing one quantity to another. The sign for ratio is **:** .

The ratio of cars to motorbikes is 3:2 or $\frac{3}{2}$.

> ○ **equivalent ratio**
>
> Equivalent ratios give the same value for each ratio when one part is compared to the other.
>
> White and blue paint that is mixed in the ratios of 2:3 and 4:6 are **equivalent ratios** so would give the same colour mix.

see also proportion

rational number *see* number

rectangle

A rectangle is a 2D shape that has four straight sides and four right angles. The opposite sides of a rectangle are equal. A square is a special type of rectangle because all 4 sides are the same length. The word rectangle is usually used to mean the oblong rectangle.

➤ rectangular

A rectangular shape is one that looks like a rectangle.

square rectangle

There are two types of rectangle.

oblong rectangle

see also oblong, quadrilateral, square

rectilinear shape

A polygon is rectilinear if it can be divided into rectangles or squares, with all the sides of the polygon meeting at right angles.

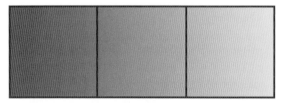

see also composite shape

recurring decimal

A recurring decimal is sometimes called a repeating decimal. It is a decimal number in which one or more of the digits keeps on repeating itself. Recurring decimals go on and on without end.

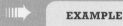

EXAMPLE

Some **recurring decimals**:

$\frac{1}{3}$ = 0.**3333333333**
The digit 3 keeps repeating.

$\frac{22}{7}$ = 3.**1428571428571**
The digits 142857 keep repeating.

see also decimal number

reduce

When you reduce something you make it smaller. You can reduce quantity or size.

OPPOSITE The opposite of reduce is enlarge or increase.

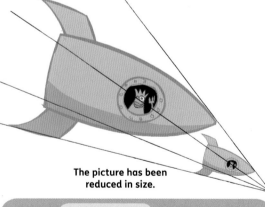

The picture has been reduced in size.

EXAMPLE

If you **reduce** 7 by 3 the answer is 4.

30 **reduced** by 2 is 15.

5 **reduced** by 10% is 4.5.

reduction

Reduction is when you write a fraction in its simplest way. Reduction is the same as simplifying a fraction.

> **EXAMPLE**
>
> $\frac{8}{12}$ can be reduced to $\frac{2}{3}$
>
> $\frac{6}{15}$ can be simplified to $\frac{2}{5}$
>
> **Reduction** of fractions is the same as simplifying.

see also fraction, simplify, cancel

reflect

If you reflect a shape you draw its mirror image. Reflecting a shape swaps left and right over.

➤ **reflection**

The mirror image of a shape is called the reflection.

object   mirror   reflection

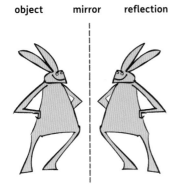

A reflection is like flipping a shape over.

see also flip, line of symmetry, symmetry, transformation

reflective symmetry
see symmetry

reflex angle *see* angle

regular polygon *see* polygon

regular polyhedron
see polyhedron

remainder (*also* r)

A remainder is what is left after you share something. In division, the remainder is the amount that is left over when you divide one number into another. The short way of writing remainder is r.

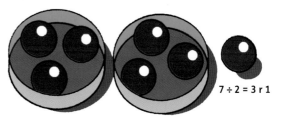

$7 \div 2 = 3\,r\,1$

see also divide, quotient, share

represent

A picture or model can be used to represent a mathematical idea to help get a clear image of it. Symbols and letters are also used to represent numbers.

> **EXAMPLE**
>
> In Roman numerals, the letter C **represents** the number 100.

➤ **representation**

A representation of a thing is something that is used to give a clear image of it, such as a picture, model, symbol or letter.

a b c d e f g h i j k l m n o p q r s t u v w x y z

reverse

① Reverse means the opposite way round or in the opposite direction. Addition and subtraction are reverse operations. Multiplication and division are also reverse operations.

② To reverse something is to turn it the other way round or make it go in the opposite direction.

▶	**EXAMPLE**

3456
If you **reverse** the digits you get 6543.

$12 + 8 - 8 = 12$

$12 \times 3 \div 3 = 12$

If you **reverse** the operation you undo what you have done.

---

see also inverse, operation

revolve

If something revolves, it turns around or moves in a circle about a certain point.

➤ **revolution**

A revolution is a complete turn about a point or axis.

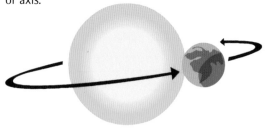

The Earth revolves around the Sun.

see also rotate, turn

rhombus

A rhombus has four equal sides. The opposite sides are parallel. It is the correct name for a diamond shape.

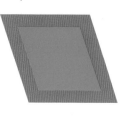

A rhombus looks like a squashed square.

see also parallelogram, quadrilateral, square

---

right angle *see* angle

---

right-angled triangle
see triangle

Roman numerals

The Romans used letters to stand for numbers. They used letters to stand for 1, 5, 10, 50, 100, 500 and 1,000.

▶			**EXAMPLE**						

I	II	III	IV	V	VI	VII	VIII	IX	X
1	2	3	4	5	6	7	8	9	10

XI	XII	XIII	XIV	XV	XVI	XVII	XVIII	XIX	XX
11	12	13	14	15	16	17	18	19	20

XL	L	C	D	M
40	50	100	500	1,000

MDLXXVI = 1,000 + 500 + 50 + 10 + 10 + 5 + 1
= 1576

---

see also C, D, I, IV, IX, L, M, V, X

rotate

If you rotate something you turn it.

➤ **rotation**

A complete rotation is four right angles or 360°.

The circle is rotating.

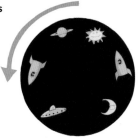

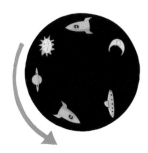

see also transformation, turn

rotational symmetry
see **symmetry**

round

❶ If something is round it is curved like a circle or sphere.

round edges

a perfectly round shape

see also circle, sphere

❷ Rounding is writing a number as an approximate. Numbers are often rounded to the nearest one, nearest ten or nearest hundred. Rounding often means rounding up or rounding down to the nearest whole number.

⮕ EXAMPLE
379 **rounded** to the nearest hundred is 400.
5.289 **rounded** to the nearest whole number is 5.
When **rounding** 136.22 **round** down to 136.
When **rounding** 45.8 km **round** up to 46 km.

see also approximate, decimal number

route

A route is the direction or path taken between two or more places. You can plan a route on a map. You can draw a route on a grid.

The dotted red line shows a route from one island to the other.

row

A row of numbers goes horizontally from side to side.

1	2	3	4
5	6	7	8
9	10	11	12

a row

see also column, horizontal

rule

❶ When you follow a rule, you follow the instructions on how to do something.
A formula is a shorthand way of writing a rule.

> **EXAMPLE**
>
> The **rule** for finding the area of a rectangle says to multiply its length by its width.

see also ruler

❷ To rule a straight line is to draw it using a ruler.

ruler

A ruler is a rectangular piece of plastic, wood or metal with measurements marked on the long straight edge. It is used to draw straight lines and to measure lengths.

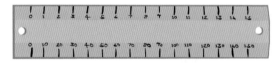

Rulers can rule lines in inches or centimetres or millimetres.

Ss

scale

A scale is a set of points on a line used for measuring. You can see a scale on maps, thermometers, measuring jugs or rulers.

0   1 km   2 km   3 km

scale: 1 cm represents 1 km

see also proportion, ratio

scale drawing

A scale drawing is smaller, larger or the same size as the real thing. Everything on a scale drawing is in proportion to the real thing.

lounge   kitchen

Scale 1:200
1 cm = 2 m

bedroom

bathroom

**Scale drawing of a small house.
Each room is in proportion to the real thing.**

see also enlarge, proportion, reduce

scalene triangle *see* triangle

second

❶ Second (2nd) is the ordinal number for two. It is the one that follows first when put in order.

see also number

❷ A second is a short length of time. There are 60 seconds in 1 minute.

clock face

The long second hand goes around the clock in 60 seconds.

see also minute, hour

---

sector *see* circle

---

segment *see* circle

---

semicircle *see* circle

---

sequence

A sequence is a set of numbers usually written in a line.

	EXAMPLE				
3	6	9	12	15	...
1	4	9	16	25	...
2	6	18	54	162	...

These are different sorts of **sequences**.

see also multiple, number

---

set

A set is a collection of numbers, shapes or objects that have something in common.

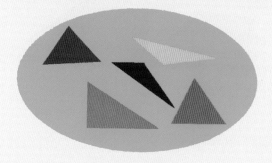

a set of triangles

○ empty set

An empty set is a set that has no members.

The set of all multiples of 4 that are odd numbers is an **empty set**.

see also attribute, property

○ subset

A subset is part of a larger set. Equilateral triangles is a subset of the set of triangles. A set can have more than one subset.

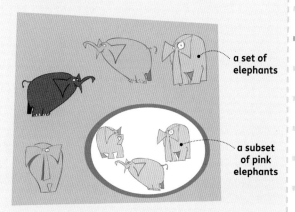

a set of elephants

a subset of pink elephants

see also sort

shallow

If something is shallow it does not go down or back a long way.

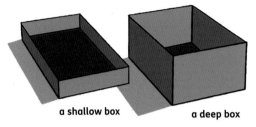

a shallow box   a deep box

see also deep

shape

A shape is made of lines and surfaces to make plane 2D shapes and solid 3D shapes.
In mathematics, the lines of shapes are usually joined to make closed shapes.

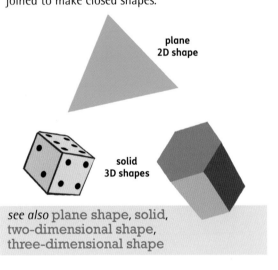

plane 2D shape

solid 3D shapes

see also plane shape, solid, two-dimensional shape, three-dimensional shape

share

When you share you divide things equally. Sharing is the same as dividing. The symbol for sharing is ÷.

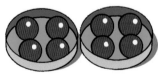

Eight shared between 2 equals 4.

8 ÷ 2 = 4

see also divide, remainder, group

side

❶ Some 2D shapes have sides. The sides can be straight or curved.

four straight sides

❷ The sides of a shape are not the top, bottom, front or back. Sides can be left or right.

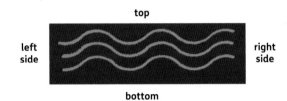

top

left side

right side

bottom

Sieve of Eratosthenes
see Eratosthenes sieve

sign

A sign is a short way of saying something.
A sign usually tells you what to do. For example, the operation signs or symbols show the type of calculation in a number problem.

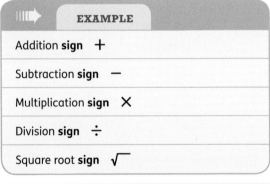

⮕	EXAMPLE
Addition **sign**	+
Subtraction **sign**	−
Multiplication **sign**	×
Division **sign**	÷
Square root **sign**	√

see also minus, plus, symbol, operation

simplest form

When a fraction is written in its simplest form, the only common factor of the numerator and denominator is 1.

EXAMPLE

$\frac{9}{12}$ can be put in its **simplest form** by dividing the numerator and denominator by 3.
The fraction $\frac{3}{4}$ is then in its **simplest form**.

see also lowest terms

simplify

To simplify you write something in a more simple way. Fractions are written in the simplest way when both numerator and denominator are as small as possible.

EXAMPLE

You can **simplify** $\frac{8}{12}$ to $\frac{2}{3}$ like this:

$$\frac{\cancel{8}^{2}}{\cancel{12}_{3}} = \frac{2}{3}$$

see also cancel, fraction

size

Size is the measure of how big an object is.
Size can also be the amount of something.
It can be the weight, volume or capacity of things.

large   small

see also dimension

slide

When you slide a shape, you move it without turning it or flipping it over. You can slide horizontally, vertically, diagonally or obliquely.

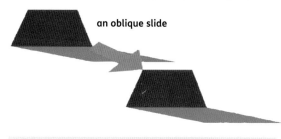

an oblique slide

see also transformation, translate

solid

A solid figure is any shape that has a length, width and height. A solid has three dimensions. Not all solids have flat faces.

some solid shapes

see also polyhedron, regular polyhedron, 3D shape

solution

A solution is an answer to a problem. Sometimes there are several solutions to a problem.

➤ **solve**

When you solve something you find the solution.

> **EXAMPLE**
>
> The **solution** to $(3 \times 4) - 2$ is 10.
>
> If you **solve** the equation $y + 7 = 10$, the **solution** is $y = 3$.

sort

When a collection of objects or set of numbers is sorted into sets, they are put into groups according to given rules.

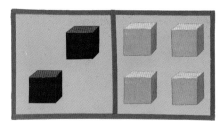

These blocks have been sorted into sets of red and yellow blocks.

see also set

span

A span is the distance from the tip of the thumb to the tip of the little finger when the fingers are stretched out.

a span

> **EXAMPLE**
>
> Two **spans** are nearly the same as one cubit.

see also cubit, palm, pace

speed

Speed is the distance travelled in a given unit of time. Speed is often measured in kilometres per hour (km/h) or miles per hour (mph).

> **EXAMPLE**
>
> The **speed** of light is about 300,000 kilometres per second which is very fast.

○ **average speed**

Average speed is a measure of the total distance travelled divided by the time taken. Speed can vary in that time, but an average speed gives a single measure.

$$\text{speed} = \frac{\text{distance}}{\text{time}}$$

A car travelling 120 km in 2 hours travels at an **average speed** of 60 km/h.

A car travels 120 kilometres in 2 hours. Its average speed will be 60 km/h.

sphere

A sphere is a perfectly round shape like a ball.

 a sphere

➤ **spherical**

Shapes that look like spheres are spherical.

spherical shapes

see also hemisphere

spiral

A spiral is a curve that goes round and round something.

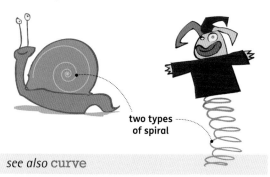

two types of spiral

see also curve

square

❶ A square is a regular polygon. It is a quadrilateral with its four sides and angles the same size.

Squares can be filled in or just an outline.

see also quadrilateral, rectangle, polygon

❷ The square of a number is the result of multiplying the number by itself.

❸ To square a number is to multiply it by itself.

EXAMPLE
The **square** of 3 is 9.
Square 3 and the answer is 9.

see also squared

square-based pyramid
see pyramid

square centimetre (*also* cm²)

A square centimetre is a unit used to measure area. It is an area that is the same as that of a 1 cm square. The short way to write square centimetre is cm².

1 cm²

A 1 cm square has an area of 1 cm².

These shapes also have an area of 1 square centimetre.

see also area, square metre, square millimetre

squared

When a number is squared, it is multiplied by itself. Whole numbers, fractions and decimals can be squared.

EXAMPLE
6 **squared** is $6 \times 6 = 36$
$6^2 = 36$
2.5 **squared** is $2.5 \times 2.5 = 6.25$
$2.5^2 = 6.25$

see also square

square metre (*also* m²)

A square metre is a unit used to measure large areas. It is an area that is the same as that of a 1 m square. The short way to write square centimetre is m².

EXAMPLE
1 **square metre** = 10,000 square centimetres
$1 m^2 = 10,000 cm^2$

see also area, square centimetre, square millimetre

a b c d e f g h i j k l m n o p q r s t u v w x y z

square millimetre (*also* mm²)

A square millimetre is a unit used to measure very small areas. It is an area that is the same as that of a 1 mm square. The short way to write square millimetre is mm².

100 mm² = 1 cm²

A 1 cm square has an area of 100 mm².

see also area, square centimetre, square metre

square number *see* number

square root

A square root of a number is the number which, multiplied by itself, gives that number. The symbol for square root is $\sqrt{\ \ }$.

EXAMPLE
$\sqrt{9} = 3$
The **square root** of 9 is 3 because $3 \times 3 = 9$.

see also number

standard unit

Standard units of measurements are units that are agreed by everyone. Metric units and imperial units are both sets of standard units.

▶ EXAMPLE
centimetre, metre, kilometre, inch, foot, mile These are some **standard units** of length.
gram, kilogram, ounce, pound These are some **standard units** of mass.
millilitre, litre, pint, gallon These are some **standard units** of capacity.

see also imperial units, metric units

star

A star can have four or more points. Extending the sides of a regular polygon will make a star. Stars are also polygons.

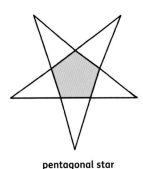

pentagonal star

hexagonal star

see also concave, polygon

statistics

Statistics is data (usually numerical) that is collected, represented in graphs or tables and analysed.

▶ EXAMPLE
'The taller you are, the further you can jump.'
How could you prove whether this is true or not?
You need to collect **statistics** to help you analyse the data and draw conclusions.

see also data

step

❶ A step is the distance between two points or two numbers.

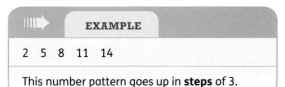

EXAMPLE

2   5   8   11   14

This number pattern goes up in **steps** of 3.

❷ When you walk, your step is the distance between your feet when you walk normally.

a step

see also pace, stride

stone

A stone is an imperial unit used to measure weight or mass. A stone weighs about 6 kilograms. Stones used to be the unit used to weigh people.

1 stone

EXAMPLE

1 **stone** = 14 pounds

1 **stone** = 14 lb

1 **stone** = 6.35 kg

see also ounce, pound

straight angle *see* angle

straight line

A straight line is the shortest distance between two points and joins those points.

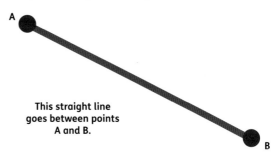

A

This straight line goes between points A and B.

B

stride

A stride is the distance from heel to toes when you take a large step.

a stride

see also pace, step

subset *see* set

a
b
c
d
e
f
g
h
i
j
k
l
m
n
o
p
q
r
s
t
u
v
w
x
y
z

subtraction

Subtraction is taking away one number from another. Subtraction gives you the difference between two numbers. It is the inverse of addition. The sign for subtraction is **−**. This is called the minus sign.

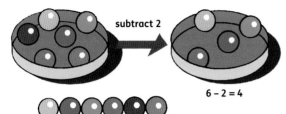

subtract 2

6 − 2 = 4

The difference between 6 and 4 is 2.

6 − 4 = 2

see also difference, minus, operation

➤ subtract

To subtract is to take one number away from another.

subtrahend

The subtrahend is a number that is subtracted from another number.

 EXAMPLE

18 − 6 = 12
18 is the minuend.
6 is the **subtrahend**.
12 is the difference.

see also difference, minuend, minus

sum

❶ The sum is the result of adding two or more numbers.

❷ To sum a set of numbers you must add them.

❸ The word sum is often used to mean a calculation using addition, subtraction, multiplication or division.

 EXAMPLE

The **sum** of 12 and 18 is 30.

Sum 12 and 18 means add 12 and 18 (12 + 18).

see also addition, plus, total

surface

A surface is a face on a shape. It has length and width but no thickness. A surface can be flat or curved.

A cylinder has two flat surfaces and one curved surface.

see also face

surface area

The surface area of a 3D shape is the total area of the outside surface.

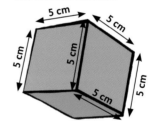

5 cm, 5 cm, 5 cm, 5 cm, 5 cm, 5 cm

The surface area of this cube is 150 cm².

Each face of the cube has an area of 25 cm².
6 × 25cm² = 150 cm²

symbol

A symbol is a sign used to stand for words. It is a mathematical shorthand way of writing something.

 EXAMPLE

CCVI   π   ÷   <   ≈   %   °C

These are all **symbols**.

see also sign

symmetry

A shape has symmetry when two or more of its parts are matching shapes. There are different types of symmetry. Plane shapes can be symmetrical about a line or have rotational symmetry about a point. Solid shapes can have symmetry about a plane or an axis.

➤ symmetrical

Something is symmetrical if one half is exactly the same as the other half but the opposite way round.

OPPOSITE The opposite of symmetrical is asymmetrical.

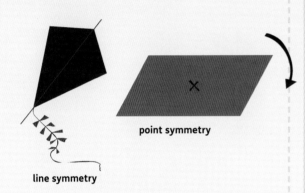

point symmetry

line symmetry

○ line symmetry

Line symmetry is sometimes called reflective or mirror symmetry. A shape has line symmetry if one half of a shape is the reflection of the other half.

see also mirror line, reflect

○ plane symmetry

Solid shapes can have plane symmetry. Plane symmetry is like mirror symmetry in flat shapes. The shape on one side of the plane must be the reflection of the other side.

see also plane

○ point symmetry

Point symmetry is when you rotate a shape about a point and it fits into its outline in a different position.

○ reflective symmetry

Reflective symmetry is sometimes called mirror symmetry. It is when one half of a shape is the reflection of the other half.

see also line of symmetry

○ rotational symmetry

Rotate a shape in its outline. If it will fit in more than one way it has rotational symmetry. If a shape being rotated looks exactly the same before the turn is complete then it has rotational symmetry.

see also order of rotational symmetry

see also line of symmetry, asymmetrical

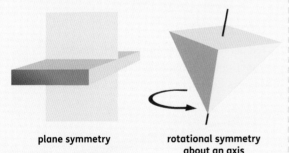

plane symmetry

rotational symmetry about an axis

reflective symmetry

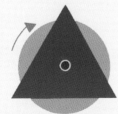
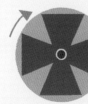

rotational symmetry about a point

table

When information is written in a list in rows and columns, it is often called a table. Multiplication facts written in order are called the multiplication tables.

a timetable

see also chart, times table

take away

To take away is to subtract or remove a number from an amount.

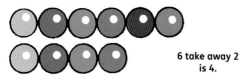

6 take away 2 is 4.

	EXAMPLE
18 **take away** 12 equals 6.
18 − 12 = 6
The − sign shows that 12 is being **taken away** from 18.

see also subtraction

tally

A tally is a mark which shows how often something happens.

tally counting

see also chart

tangram

A tangram is a puzzle made up of triangles, a square, and a rhombus cut out of a square. The tangram pieces can be used to make new shapes.

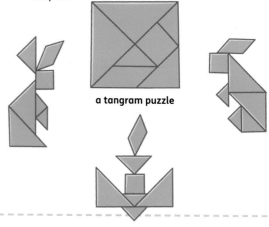

a tangram puzzle

temperature

Temperature is a measure of the heat of something, or how cold it is. It is measured in degrees Celsius (°C) or degrees Fahrenheit (°F).

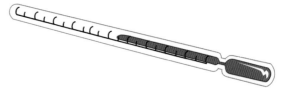

	EXAMPLE
A thermometer is used to measure the **temperature**. Today the **temperature** outside is 18°C.

see also Celsius, Fahrenheit

tenth

❶ One-tenth ($\frac{1}{10}$) is a fraction showing a whole divided into 10 equal parts.

> **EXAMPLE**
>
> A millimetre is one-**tenth** of a centimetre.
>
> 1 mm = $\frac{1}{10}$ cm
>
> 10 mm = 1 cm

❷ Tenth (10th) is an ordinal number showing the 10th position.

tessellate

When you tessellate, you fit shapes together into a pattern without leaving any gaps between the shapes. Triangles and quadrilaterals will always tessellate.

➤ **tessellation**

Tessellation is a tiling pattern in which shapes are fitted together without leaving any gaps between the shapes.

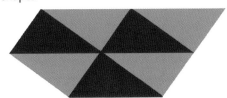

a tessellation of triangles

see also pattern

tetrahedron

(*plural* tetrahedra)

A tetrahedron is a solid shape with four sides. Each side is a triangle. The regular tetrahedron has faces that are equilateral triangles.

a regular tetrahedron

see also polyhedron, pyramid

thousandth

❶ One-thousandth ($\frac{1}{1,000}$) is a fraction showing a whole divided into 1,000 equal parts.

> **EXAMPLE**
>
> A millilitre is one-**thousandth** of a litre.
>
> 1,000 ml = 1 litre

❷ Thousandth (1,000th) is an ordinal number showing the 1,000th position.

three-dimensional shape

Three-dimensional shapes are solid shapes. They have length, width and height. 3D is short for three-dimensional.

three-dimensional shapes

see also polyhedron, solid

time

Time is how long something lasts. It is measured in units such as seconds, minutes, hours, days, weeks, months and years. Clocks and watches are used to tell the time. Stopwatches and timers are used to measure time.

In 1 hour's time it will be 4:30.

> **EXAMPLE**
>
> A second is a short **time**.
>
> A century is a long **time**.

see also a.m., p.m., timer

timer

A timer is an instrument used to measure time. Sand timers, stopwatches, pendulums, clocks and watches are all different types of timer.

These are timers.

times

Times is how often an addition is to be done. It means the same as 'multiplied by' and the symbol is **×**.

4 **times** 3 = 4 + 4 + 4 = 20

4 × 3 = 12

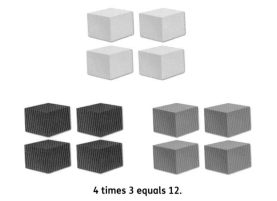

4 times 3 equals 12.

4 × 3 = 12

see also multiplication

times table

A times table is a list of multiplication facts for a particular number put in order. The multiples of the number are often written or spoken from 1 to 12.

This is the start of the 6 **times table**:

$1 \times 6 = 6$

$2 \times 6 = 12$

$3 \times 6 = 18$

$4 \times 6 = 24$

$5 \times 6 = 30$

title

A title tells you the name of something or what something is about. A title is a type of label.

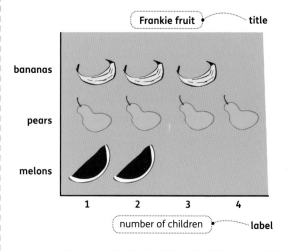

Frankie fruit ······ title

bananas

pears

melons

1   2   3   4

number of children ····· label

see also label

ton

A ton is an imperial unit used to measure mass or weight. It is a very heavy weight weighing about 1,000 kg.

▶ EXAMPLE
1 **ton** = 2,240 pounds
1 **ton** = 2,240 lb
1 **ton** = 1,016 kg

see also imperial units, metric ton, tonne

tonne

A tonne is a metric unit used to measure mass or weight. A tonne equals 1,000 kilograms. A tonne is sometimes called a metric ton.

▶ EXAMPLE
1 **tonne** = 1,000 kilograms
1 **tonne** = 1,000 kg

see also kilogram, metric units, ton

top-heavy fraction *see* fraction

total

❶ A total is found by adding all the numbers together. A total is the sum of numbers.
❷ To total a set of numbers is to add them up.

▶ EXAMPLE
The **total** of 12, 14 and 20 is 46.
Total 12, 14 and 20 means 12 + 14 + 20.

see also addition, sum

transformation

A transformation is a way of moving a shape or an object. Three commonly used transformations are turn (rotation), slide (translation), and flip (reflection).

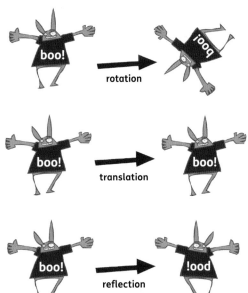

rotation

translation

reflection

see also reflect, rotate, translate

translate

If you translate a shape you slide it to a different position. You do not turn or rotate the shape.

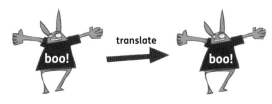

translate

➤ **translation**

A translation is when you slide a shape to a different position.

see also slide, transformation

trapezium (*plural* trapezia)

A trapezium is a four-sided shape that has one pair of sides that are parallel. The other two sides are not parallel.

| trapezium | right-angled trapezium | isosceles trapezium |

see also **parallel, quadrilateral**

treble

❶ If you treble something, you multiply it by three.
❷ Treble is three times as much in size or amount.

EXAMPLE

10 **trebled** is 30.

Treble 6 is 18.

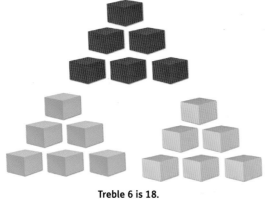

Treble 6 is 18.

$6 \times 3 = 18$

see also **double**

tree diagram *see* diagram

trial

A trial is an experiment, for example rolling a dice or tossing a coin to discover the outcome.

see also **event, probability, random**

trial-and-improvement

Trial-and-improvement is a way of finding the solution of a problem through making sensible guesses.

EXAMPLE

What number must be added to 14 to give an answer of 22?

$14 + ? = 22$

First guess could be 9, but $14 + 9 = 23$ which is bigger than 22.

Second guess could be using a number smaller than 9 like 7, but $14 + 7 = 21$ which is smaller than 22.

The next guess must be bigger than 7, but smaller than 9, so try 8.

$14 + 8 = 22$

triangle

A triangle is a polygon that has three sides.
The three angles of a triangle add up to 180°.
All triangles will tessellate. The words equilateral,
isosceles and scalene tell you about the sides
of a triangle. The words acute, obtuse, and
right-angled tell you about the angles of
a triangle.

➤ **triangular**
A triangular shape has three sides.

⚙ acute-angled triangle

An acute-angled triangle has all three angles
less than a right angle.

⚙ equilateral triangle

An equilateral triangle has all its sides the
same length. Each of its three angles is also
the same.

⚙ isosceles triangle

An isosceles triangle has two sides that are
the same length. Two angles are also equal.

⚙ obtuse-angled triangle

An obtuse-angled triangle has one angle
greater than a right angle.

⚙ right-angled triangle

A right-angled triangle contains one right
angle. Right-angled triangles can be isosceles
or scalene.

see also right angle

⚙ scalene triangle

A scalene triangle has no sides the same
length. All its angles are a different size.

see also polygon, tessellate

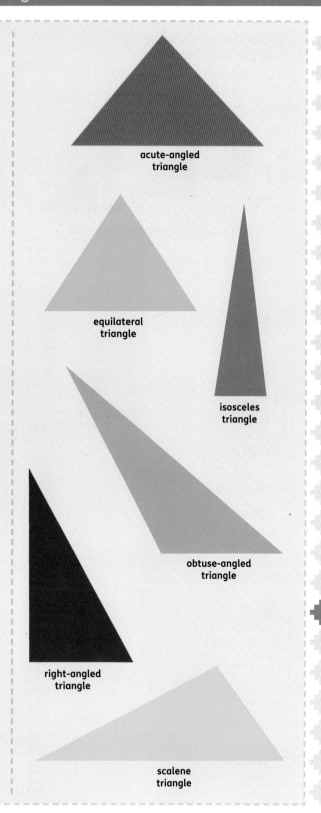

acute-angled
triangle

equilateral
triangle

isosceles
triangle

obtuse-angled
triangle

right-angled
triangle

scalene
triangle

a b c d e f g h i j k l m n o p q r s t u v w x y z

triangular numbers
(*also* triangle numbers)

Triangular numbers are 1, 3, 6, 10, 15, 21 . . .
The difference between neighbouring triangular
numbers increases by 1 each time.

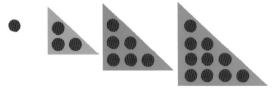

Triangular numbers make a triangle pattern.

triangular prism *see* prism

triangular pyramid *see* pyramid

triple
Triple means three times as much in size or amount.

> **IIID** **EXAMPLE**
>
> **Triple** 5 is 15.

see also double, treble

turn
When something turns it spins, rotates, revolves
or whirls.

**A quarter, a half turn and a full turn
in a clockwise direction.**

see also anticlockwise, clockwise,
revolve, rotate, transformation

two-dimensional shape
Two-dimensional shapes are flat shapes.
They have length and width but no thickness.
2D is short for two-dimensional.

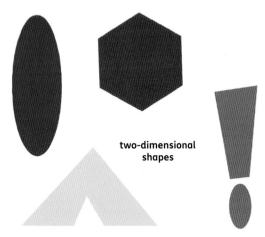

**two-dimensional
shapes**

see also flat shape, polygon,
plane shape

unequal

If two things are unequal they are not equal. The sign for not equal to is ≠.

> **EXAMPLE**
>
> 3 × 8 ≠ 25
>
> 3 × 8 = 24

see also equal

unit

❶ Unit is a name for 'one'. Hundreds, tens and units or ones are used in place value.

> **EXAMPLE**
>
> # 143
>
> 3 is in the position of **units**.
> 4 is in the position of tens.
> 1 is in the position of hundreds.

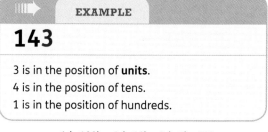

1 (× 100)   4 (× 10)   3 (× 1) = 143

Hundreds (10 × 10)	Tens (10s)	Units (1s)

see also place value, base

❷ Units are used in measuring. Metres are units used to measure length.

> **EXAMPLE**
>
> Litre is a **unit** of capacity.
>
> Kilogram is a **unit** of mass.
>
> Kilometre is a **unit** of distance.

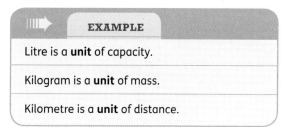

a litre

1,000 ml
800
600
400
200
0

see also imperial units, metric units, standard unit

unit fraction *see* fraction

unlike fractions *see* fraction

Vv

V

The Romans used the letter V to stand for the number 5.

> **EXAMPLE**
>
> **I V X L C D M**
>
> | V | = | 5 |
> |---|---|---|
> | VI | = | 6 |
> | VII | = | 7 |

see also **Roman numerals**

value

The value of something is what it is worth.

> **EXAMPLE**
>
> **143**
>
> The digit 3 has the **value** of 3.
> The digit 4 has the **value** of 40.
> The digit 1 has the **value** of 100.
>
> The **value** of $(7 + 3) \times 4$ is 40.

see also **place value**

variable

A variable is an unknown number in an equation that can take different values, usually shown by a symbol or letter.

> **EXAMPLE**
>
> In the equation $3x + y = 12$ the letters x and y are both **variables**.

see also **constant**

Venn diagram see **diagram**

vertex (*plural* vertices)

A vertex is a point at which two or more lines meet in an object or a shape.

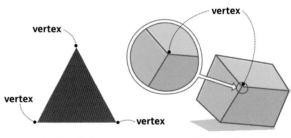

vertex

vertex

vertex

vertex

vertex

A triangle has three vertices.

This box has eight vertices.

vertical

A vertical line is at right angles to a horizontal line. A vertical line goes up and down.

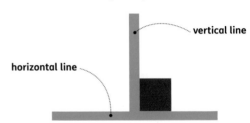

vertical line

horizontal line

Vertical and horizontal lines meet at 90°.

see also **perpendicular**

volume

Volume is the amount of space taken up by a solid shape. When measuring volume, cubic units such as cm³ and m³ are used.

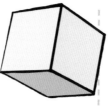

 EXAMPLE

A 1 cm cube has a **volume** of
1 cm × 1 cm × 1 cm = 1 cm³.

A 2 cm cube has a **volume** of
2 cm × 2 cm × 2 cm = 8 cm³.

see also capacity, cubic centimetre, cubic metre

vote

If you vote, you are given a choice and you choose which you want. The thing with most votes is the favourite.

Most people voted for the wig party.

see also tally

vulgar fraction *see* fraction

week

A week is a period of 7 days. There are 52 weeks in a year.

see also day, year, month

weigh

You weigh something to find out how heavy it is. To weigh something you use a balance or scales.

You can weigh yourself using scales.

see also mass, weight

weight

Weight is the heaviness of something. Weight is the force with which an object is pulled towards the centre of the Earth. The word weight is often used instead of mass although they are not quite the same.

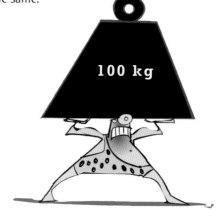

100 kg

see also mass

whole number *see* number

width

The width is the distance from one side to the other and is sometimes called the breadth. When measuring length and width, the width is usually the shorter distance.

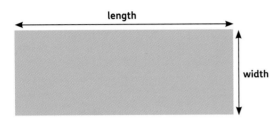

length

width

see also breadth, length

X

The Romans used the letter X to stand for the number 10.

EXAMPLE						
I	V	X	L	C	D	M
X = 10						
XI = 11						
XII = 12						

see also Roman numerals

x-axis *see* axis

x-coordinate *see* coordinate

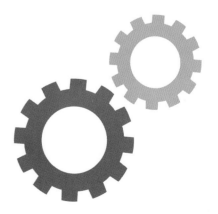

Yy

yard

A yard is an imperial unit used to measure distance. There are three feet in one yard. A yard is about 90 cm.

> **EXAMPLE**
>
> 1 **yard** = 3 feet
>
> 1 **yard** = 36 inches
>
> 1 **yard** = 91.44 cm

see also foot, imperial units, inch

y-axis *see* axis

y-coordinate *see* coordinate

year

A year is how long it takes the Earth to make a revolution around the Sun. It takes just over 365 days for the Earth to travel around the Sun. Every fourth year is a leap year.

> **EXAMPLE**
>
> 1 **year** = 365 days
>
> 1 leap **year** = 366 days
>
> 1 **year** = 12 months

see also calendar, leap year, month

Zz

zero

Zero is the number 0. It is is an integer that separates positive and negative numbers. Zeros are used to show the place value of other digits in larger numbers. Zero is also another word for nothing or nought.

$$-4 \quad -3 \quad -2 \quad -1 \quad 0 \quad 1 \quad 2 \quad 3 \quad 4$$

Zero separates positive and negative numbers.

> **EXAMPLE**
>
> $5 - 5 = \mathbf{0}$
>
> $5 \times \mathbf{0} = \mathbf{0}$
>
> 5   50   **500**   **5000**
> The **zeros** change the value of the digit 5.

see also integer, place value, nought

a b c d e f g h i j k l m n o p q r s t u v w x y z

117

Shapes

2D

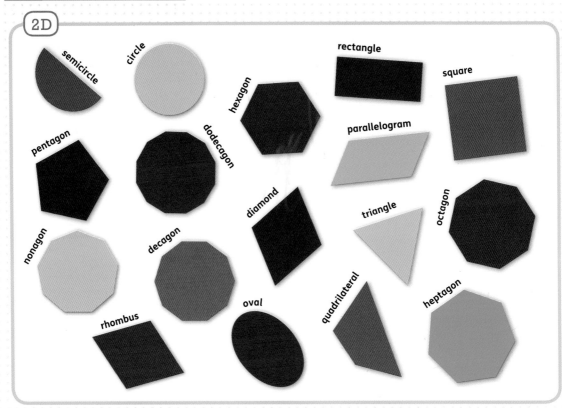

semicircle
circle
rectangle
square
hexagon
parallelogram
pentagon
dodecagon
nonagon
decagon
diamond
triangle
octagon
rhombus
oval
quadrilateral
heptagon

3D

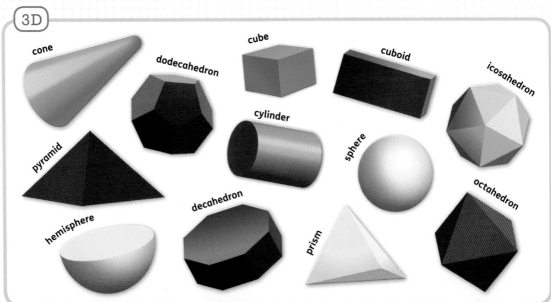

cone
cube
cuboid
dodecahedron
icosahedron
cylinder
pyramid
sphere
hemisphere
decahedron
prism
octahedron

Useful mathematical tables

LENGTH
10 millimetres (mm) = 1 centimetre (cm)
10 centimetres (cm) = 1 decimetre (dm)
10 decimetres (dm) = 1 metre (m)
1,000 metres (m) = 1 kilometre (km)

WEIGHT, MASS
1,000 grams (g) = 1 kilogram (kg)
1,000 kilograms (kg) = 1 tonne (t)

CAPACITY
10 millilitres (ml) = 1 centilitre (cl)
10 centilitres (cl) = 1 decilitre (dl)
10 decilitres (dl) = 1 litre (l)

VOLUME
1,000 cubic millimetres (mm^3) = 1 cubic centimetre (cm^3)
1,000 cubic centimetres (cm^3) = 1 cubic decimetre (dm^3)
1,000 cubic decimetres (dm^3) = 1 cubic metre (m^3)

AREA
100 square millimetres (mm^2) =
1 square centimetre (cm^2)

100 square centimetres (cm^2) =
1 square decimetre (dm^2)

100 square decimetres (dm^2) =
1 square metre (m^2)

1,000,000 square metres (m^2) =
1 square kilometre (km^2)

TIME
60 seconds (sec) = 1 minute (min)
60 minutes (min) = 1 hour (h)
24 hours (h) = 1 day
7 days = 1 week

52 weeks = 1 year
365 days = 1 year
366 days = 1 leap year
12 months = 1 year

10 years = 1 decade
100 years = 1 century
1,000 years = 1 millennium

Useful mathematical formulae

PERIMETER
perimeter of a quadrilateral = sum of all 4 sides
perimeter of a triangle = sum of all 3 sides
perimeter (circumference) of a circle = 2πr (2 × π × r)

AREA
area of a quadrilateral = l × w (length × width)
area of a triangle = $\frac{1}{2}$ × b × h ($\frac{1}{2}$ × base × height)
area of a circle = πr^2 (π × radius squared)

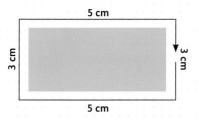

5 cm
3 cm
3 cm
5 cm

The perimeter of this rectangle is 16 cm.

The area of this rectangle is 15 cm^2.

The area of this triangle is 7 cm^2.

The perimeter of this triangle is 12 cm.

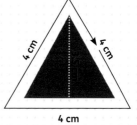

4 cm
4 cm
4 cm

Time

These are different ways of telling the time.

9:00

nine o'clock

9:05

five past nine

9:10

ten past nine

9:15

nine fifteen
quarter past nine

9:20

nine twenty
twenty past nine

9:25

nine twenty-five

9:30

nine thirty
half past nine

9:35

nine thirty-five
twenty-five to ten

9:40

nine forty
twenty to ten

9:45

nine forty-five
quarter to ten

9:50

nine fifty
ten to ten

9:55

nine fifty-five
five to ten

12:00

midday (noon)

24:00

midnight

Time and fractions

You can use fractions to measure time.

quarter of an hour

$$\frac{1}{4} = \frac{15}{60}$$

15 minutes is $\frac{1}{4}$ of an hour.

You can also say $\frac{1}{4}$ of 60 minutes is 15 minutes.

half an hour

$$\frac{1}{4} + \frac{1}{4} = \frac{1}{2}$$

$$\frac{1}{2} = \frac{30}{60}$$

30 minutes is $\frac{1}{2}$ an hour.

You can also say $\frac{1}{2}$ of 60 minutes is 30 minutes.

three quarters of an hour

$$\frac{1}{4} + \frac{1}{4} + \frac{1}{4} = \frac{3}{4}$$

$$\frac{1}{2} + \frac{1}{4} = \frac{3}{4}$$

$$\frac{3}{4} = \frac{45}{60}$$

45 minutes is $\frac{3}{4}$ of an hour.

You can also say $\frac{3}{4}$ of 60 minutes is 45 minutes.

Instruction words and phrases

These words tell you what to do when you work on a number problem in class, in a test or for homework.

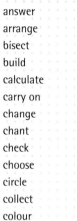

answer	discuss	order
arrange	draw	place
bisect	estimate	plot
build	exchange	predict
calculate	experiment	present
carry on	explain	prove
change	fill in	put
chant	find	rearrange
check	finish	record
choose	fold	repeat
circle	identify	represent
collect	interpret	shade
colour	investigate	sketch
compare	join	solve
complete	join in	split
construct	join up	tally
continue	justify	tick
convert	listen	trace
cost	look at	turn
count	make	use
decide	match	write
describe	name	

SOME COMMON PHRASES IN MATHS

check your work	how much?	show your method
count back	in the text	start at
count on	on the line	start from
count to	pick out	start with
cross out	point to	tell me
follow the instruction	show how	work out
how many?	show me	

Chance words

When you talk about the chance of something happening, you can use these words to say whether you think it will definitely happen or not happen, or whether it is somewhere in the middle.

biased	likely	evens	equally likely
doubtful	possible	odds	chance
impossible	probably	least common	equal chance
uncertain	maybe	least popular	even chance
unfair	random	most common	fifty-fifty chance
unlikely	likelihood	most popular	
	possibility	rare	

certain

definitely

fair

certainly

Money words

These are words you can use to talk about money, whether you are solving money problems in class or planning how to spend your money.

discount	buy, buying, buys, bought	cheap, cheaper, cheapest	change
gain	cost	costs less	coin
interest	pay	costs more	note
interest rate	sell, sold	dear, dearer, dearest	
loss	spend, spent	expensive	
price	cost price	least expensive	
profit	selling price	most expensive	
value			

Position and direction words

These are words you can use to describe the position of objects or places. You can say where they are in relation to each other or to you.

above

across — beside

after — behind — forward — left

along — between — from — middle

apart — bottom — half way — near

backward — close to — in — next to

before — down — in front — off

below — far — inside — on

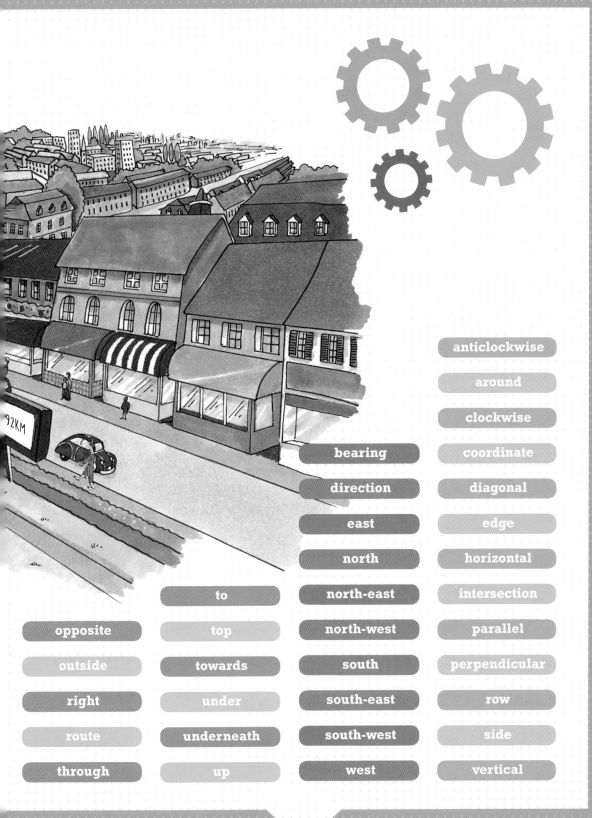

anticlockwise

around

clockwise

bearing

coordinate

direction

diagonal

east

edge

north

horizontal

to

north-east

intersection

opposite

top

north-west

parallel

outside

towards

south

perpendicular

right

under

south-east

row

route

underneath

south-west

side

through

up

west

vertical

92KM

Apparatus

These are things you might use in the classroom.

ABACUS

DIGIT CARDS

BALANCE
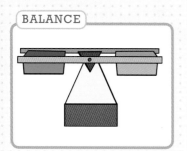

CALCULATOR

EQUALISER
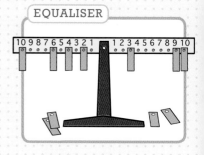

DICE

GEOBOARD
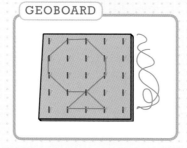

INTERLOCKING CUBES
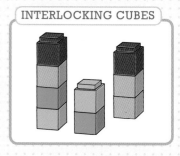

NUMBER RODS
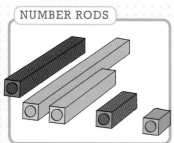

MEASURING JUG
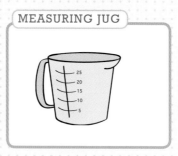

PEGBOARD
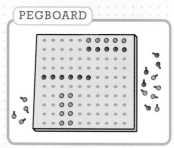

NUMBER CARDS

NUMBER FAN

SAND TIMER

HEIGHT MEASURER

COMPASS

NUMBER SHAPES

SCALES

SPRING BALANCE

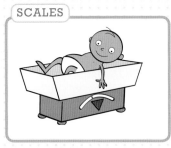

MEASURING CYLINDER

TRUNDLE WHEEL

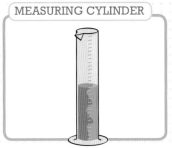

METRE STICK

TOCKERS

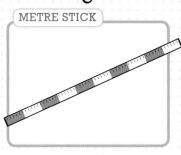

STOP WATCH

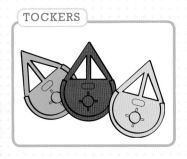

SET SQUARE

PROTRACTOR

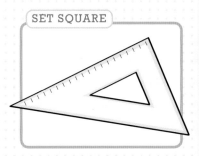

SURVEYOR'S TAPE

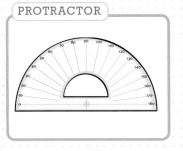

INTERLOCKING SHAPES

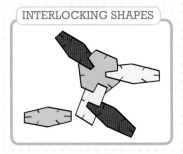

For more vocabulary and language skills:

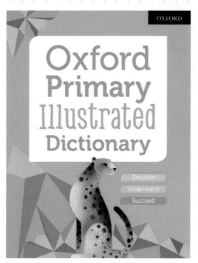

age 8+

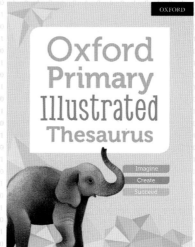

age 8+

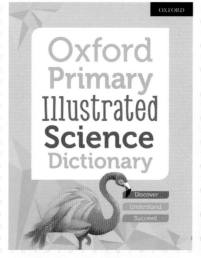

age 8+

age 8+